THE UNDERGROUND GOURMET COOKBOOK

MILTON GLASER AND JEROME SNYDER

EDITED BY JOYCE ZONANA

SIMON AND SCHUSTER, NEW YORK

Designed by Milton Glaser
Manufactured in the United States of America

1 2 3 4 5 6 7 8 9 10

Library of Congress Cataloging in Publication Data

Glaser, Milton.
    The underground gourmet cookbook.

    Includes index.
    1. Cookery, International.   2. New York (City)—Restaurants—Directories.
I. Snyder, Jerome, joint author.   II. Title.
TX725.A1G43   641.5′9   75-19299
ISBN 0-671-22076-4

ACKNOWLEDGMENTS

In essence this book, with its personal recipes, is a collective acknowledgment of the generous help proffered by the good people who make up the list of contributors. We would, however, like to use this space for a special thanks to all the men and women included in this book who took the time despite pressing kitchen duties to talk with us. They explained their style and procedures very often in the face of immense language difficulties. They would supplement words with practical demonstrations of unclear steps and techniques and always with virtually parental concern and unfailing good humor.

Among the many friends and associates who helped along the way, Ms. Judith Eisenberg and Ms. Susan Lasky deserve special mention for their observations, criticisms and ever-courageous palates. Finally, a rose for Ms. Nelly Zonana, who gave us the motherly benefit of at least forty years of good cooking both here and in her native Egypt.

MILTON GLASER
JEROME SNYDER
JOYCE ZONANA

CONTENTS

INTRODUCTION

Just about ten years ago, an innocent conversation without any apparent portent took place on the corner of 31st Street and Lexington Avenue. That corner provided a likely place for chance meetings and the attendant small talk, since our respective studios were only a few steps away. This day's casual corner exchange, however, did lead to an insight of more significance than we had at first imagined. The subject of the discussion was restaurants—good, cheap and generally unrecognized. We were trying to outdo each other with our personal knowledge of where these finds were tucked away in the city, and as we continued to match our special discoveries— restaurant for restaurant, eating place for eating place—we realized that information of this sort had never been gathered into any formal collection or book. Restaurant reviews at that time were directed virtually without exception toward those establishments grouped in the moderately priced to expensive range. The plain-to-see yet ignored fact was that the greater-numbered followers of good food were more interested in eating well yet inexpensively, getting their money's worth and perhaps adding a certain measure of adventure to their gastronomic pursuit.

Thus, the idea of some sort of compendium filling that badly overlooked need was born there on the sidewalks of New York. Although our credentials were better known in the graphic than in the culinary arts, we were not entirely without some of the qualities or capabilities necessary for the task. We both were and are amateur cooks; we are native New Yorkers; we were traumatized by the Depression (the former and famous); we have good noses for a bargain; and last and certainly not least, we both have cast-iron—or should we say stainless-steel—stomachs. The unparalleled ethnic diversity of New York offered us a seeming abundance of good, cheap interesting eating places. We began by pooling our knowledge and walking the streets in search of the city's yet undiscovered cornucopia. The ultimate aim was to put our findings into a guide—one that eventually became *The Underground Gourmet* or, as the first edition's subtitle read, "How to Eat Well in New York for Under $2.00 and As Low As 50 Cents."

Economic conditions have since relegated that possibility to history. The inevitable pocket adjustment was made in a subsequently revised edition moving things up to $3.00, and one more now in progress brings eating up to the $4.00 mark and somewhat above; yet despite inflation's irresistible shove, the values and bargains still remain. Some of the pieces in the book first appeared in the Sunday supplement of the now defunct *Herald Tribune*. Probably the most memorable was a comparison between Yonah Schimmel's authentic Old World knish and the current commercial parvenu potato imitation. Another article cleared up some of the mystery and strangeness of a popular Puerto Rican snack, the cuchifrito. Still another piece represented the first major acknowledgment of Soul food in the nonblack press.

But all that was some ten years ago, and since then the Underground Gourmet adventure has gone on in weekly style as a regular column in *New York* magazine. During all those years we've eaten dreadful food and excellent food and have met some marvelous people who nobly cook and serve. Many of the restaurants in which they ply their profession are landmarks; others, more ephemeral, come and go for a variety of reasons. Even some mentioned in this book will have vanished during the time between research and publication.

Many years back, we reached the now obvious conclusion that New York's good, cheap restaurants deserved more than casually spoken recognition. We now feel that the record demands a more durable place for the ways and means used in preparing their good food and great dishes. In collecting these recipes for some

of the finest and most unusual dishes we've encountered, we hope
to further the love and lore of the good, cheap restaurants and to
document in somewhat more lasting form the contributions these
small institutions have made to enhancing New York life and
culture.

One of the difficulties in gathering these recipes was peculiar
to the broad ethnic nature of the New York restaurant. Chefs
were not always fluent in English, and a culinarily knowledgeable
linguistic go-between in myriad native tongues was not readily at
hand. Then too, restaurant chefs in their daily alchemy seldom if
ever measure ingredients in the way we've come to expect from
cookbooks. Professional cooks use experience, imagination and,
of course, taste as their personal guides. Recording these recipes
also proved to be in many cases a process of articulating the in-
articulate, making explicit the techniques and judgments that are
instinctive to the people who use them. In that aim we trust we
have been faithful to the chef's spirit as well as to his or her
directions.

THE
UNDERGROUND
GOURMET
COOKBOOK

AKASAKA

715 SECOND AVENUE
NEW YORK CITY
867-6410

The food at Akasaka is remarkably pristine in appearance and flavor, like the restaurant's electric blue-and-white decor.

S. Yamamoto, the restaurant's manager, was extremely helpful in explaining the following dishes to us, although he insisted that experience was an essential factor in Japanese cuisine. The recipes below are simple enough to be easily reproduced at home; any unusual ingredients may be purchased at Katagiri, a Japanese grocery at 224 East 59th Street.

KAKIAGE (SERVES 2)

2 large onions, chopped
2 eggs
1 cup chopped shrimp (peeled and deveined)
½ cup white flour
   water

   oil for frying (3 parts vegetable oil to 1 part olive oil)

Combine the first four ingredients, adding just enough water to hold mixture together. Shape into two patties and deep-fry in vegetable-and-olive-oil mixture. Oil should be at only 250°. Turn patty over once during cooking and fry just until golden brown. Serve with Tempura Sauce.

TEMPURA SAUCE

1   quart water
1   2½-inch piece of kombu
¼   cup bonito flakes
¼   cup soy sauce
¼   cup rice wine (Mirin)
1   teaspoon chopped ginger
1   teaspoon grated horseradish

Bring water and kombu to boil. Add bonito flakes and simmer for 5 minutes. Strain and conserve liquid, which is called "dashi." Discard kombu and bonito.

Combine 1 cup dashi with soy sauce and Mirin. Serve Kakiage with Tempura Sauce and ginger and horseradish in small bowls.

SUSHI RICE

1   cup Japanese white rice (Kotobuki or Kokuho brand)
1½/10   cups water
⅓   cup rice vinegar
1   teaspoon salt
1   tablespoon sugar

Place rice and water in pot. Cover, bring to a boil and simmer 20 to 30 minutes, until rice is soft. Add vinegar, salt and sugar, and mix well. Refrigerate and serve cold with raw fish and seaweed.

FUTOMAKI (SERVES 1)

bamboo rolling mat ($11 \times 7\frac{1}{2}$ inches)

1 piece of nori, approximately 8×8 inches
Sushi Rice
boiled spinach
fresh sliced vegetables (cucumber, scallion, pepper)
boiled shrimp
pieces of omelet

Place seaweed on mat. Press a $\frac{1}{2}$-inch layer of cold Sushi Rice onto seaweed. Cover with assorted vegetables, shrimp and omelet. Using mat, roll seaweed tight around the rice. Slice into 10 cylindrical sections and serve.

AKI DINING ROOM

420 WEST 119TH STREET
NEW YORK CITY
UN 4-5970

The Aki Dining Room is a gracious, quiet restaurant located on the first floor of an Upper West Side apartment building. Though the room is rather large, one feels that one is in a residence rather than a place of business, which adds to the charm of eating there. The food is professionally prepared and served, under the direction of owner Arthur Shiwotsuka.

Mr. Shiwotsuka, born of Japanese parents in the United States, is quite an enterprising man. In addition to Aki he owns another restaurant and two Japanese groceries. The most recently opened store is just across the George Washington Bridge in Fort Lee and caters primarily to the affluent Japanese community that is developing in New Jersey. The store, also named Aki, carries a large selection of Oriental foods. It is a well-organized and inviting place, and the staff is helpful and informative.

TERIYAKI (SERVES 4)

¾ cup soy sauce
¼ cup sugar
¾ cup sake
1 pound filleted salmon, tuna, striped bass or mackerel

Combine soy, sugar and sake. Marinate fish in this mixture for 30 minutes.

Broil one side of fish for 4 minutes, turn and broil the second side for 6 minutes. Baste with sauce three times during the broiling. Serve hot, sprinkled with sauce.

YAKITORI (SERVES 4)

¾ cup soy sauce
¼ cup sugar
¾ cup sake
1 3-to-4-pound chicken, boned and cut into 1½-inch cubes
10 large scallions, cut in 2-inch lengths
  sansho or cayenne pepper

Combine soy, sugar and sake. Mix well.

Skewer pieces of chicken and scallion alternately on 6-inch skewers. Baste with sauce and broil, basting with more sauce several times during the cooking, until chicken is done (about 10 minutes). Serve immediately, sprinkled with sansho or cayenne.

TEMPURA (SERVES 4)

1 pound large green shrimp
1 pound assorted fresh vegetables (string beans, eggplant, parsley, etc.)
1 egg
1 cup water
1⅛ cups flour

  oil for deep frying

¼ cup soy sauce
½ cup Dashi (see below)
2 teaspoons sugar
  pinch MSG

  freshly grated daikon or radish
  freshly grated horseradish
  freshly grated ginger

Shell shrimp, leaving tail fins attached to the flesh. Devein, and slit undersection of shrimp to prevent excessive curling. Wash and dry thoroughly. Wash and dry vegetables, and cut into pieces the same size as the shrimp.

Beat egg and water. Add flour and mix lightly. Two or three stirs should be enough, even though some lumps remain.

Heat oil for deep frying. Dip shrimp and vegetables one at a time into batter, then drop into oil. Large bubbles will form. When they become small, the Tempura is ready. Drain and serve, with sauce and condiments.

For sauce, combine soy, Dashi, sugar and MSG. Heat briefly. Place daikon, horseradish and ginger in small dishes. Individual diners add as much of these as desired to the sauce, into which the tempura is dipped.

DASHI

1 ½-inch-square piece of kombu (seaweed)
½ cup bonito flakes
2½ cups water

Place kombu in water and bring to a boil; then remove kombu and reserve. Add bonito flakes to water. Remove from heat and let steep a minute or two. Strain liquid and reserve bonito flakes. Discard liquid.

  kombu and bonito flakes from above
⅙ cup bonito flakes
1½ cups water

Place kombu and bonito in water. Bring to boil and remove from heat. Strain and conserve liquid, "dashi." Discard bonito and kombu.

Jerry Lopez, heir to Al and Bess's tiny domain, stands beside his cash register.

ALANBESS LUNCHEONETTE

226 WEST 37TH STREET
NEW YORK CITY
OX 5-7474

Alanbess remains, but Al and Bess Rappaport—the lunch-eonette's inimitable founders—are gone. They've retired after 42 years' dedication to their 11-stool counter operation, and the garment district will never be the same. Jerry Lopez, who worked with the Rappaports for nearly 20 years, has taken over the business, which is still thriving.

The Chicken Scampi below is a Rappaport family favorite, developed over 30 years ago. The quantities specified add up to a very tasty dish, but don't hesitate to throw in more garlic or onion. Bess suggested that you add fresh garlic at the end; Al said no. They agreed, however, that the flavor improves with age, and that Perdue chickens are the best.

CHICKEN SCAMPI ("SERVES 2 HEAVY EATERS OR 4 NORMAL PEOPLE")

1 3-pound frying chicken, cut into 16 pieces
1 tablespoon coarse salt
1 cup good-quality olive oil
1 pound onions, chopped
6 cloves garlic, minced
1 heaping teaspoon oregano
1 teaspoon basil
⅛ teaspoon red pepper

1 teaspoon salt
¾ cup chopped fresh parsley
6 heaping tablespoons Italian-seasoned bread crumbs
½ cup chopped scallions
8 tablespoons grated Parmesan cheese
1 pound linguine (Ronzoni #17)

Wash chicken well. Dry, sprinkle with coarse salt and let stand.

In a large, heavy pot, sauté onions in 3 tablespoons oil until translucent. Add garlic and sauté another minute or two. Do not let onions or garlic brown. Remove to small bowl.

Arrange chicken in same pot, placing large pieces on the bottom. Add balance of oil, plus oregano, basil, pepper, salt and ½ cup parsley. Cover and simmer gently for 25 minutes.

Add sautéed onion and garlic to chicken, stir, and simmer another 15 minutes.

Stir bread crumbs into sauce. Serve chicken and sauce over boiled linguine. Garnish with scallions, remaining parsley and Parmesan.

At Alanbess, the chicken is served boned, and you might want to do the same at home. But you probably won't, and the bones don't hurt the flavor at all. Just dig in and eat with your hands. It's messy but good.

HARTFORD CHOWDER (SERVES 6 TO 8)

2 medium onions, chopped
2 strips bacon, cut into small pieces
3 quarts water
2 carrots, diced
2 stalks celery, diced
2 large potatoes, diced

1 pound stewed tomatoes
2 tablespoons thyme
  salt and pepper to taste
1 dozen large clams, diced
  juice from clams
2 heaping tablespoons cornstarch
½ cup cold water
1 pint light cream

In a large pot, sauté onions with bacon until onions are golden.
Add 3 quarts water, vegetables, thyme, salt and pepper. Bring
to a boil, cover and simmer 1 hour.

Add clams with their juice, and simmer another 15 minutes.
Remove 2 cups of broth and let cool.

Blend cornstarch and ½ cup cold water until smooth. Add
to cooled broth. Add cream to this mixture and blend well.

Add mixture of cream, broth and cornstarch to rapidly boiling soup, stirring constantly so that it does not curdle. Remove
from heat immediately, adjust seasoning and serve.

DIETETIC PINEAPPLE-BLUEBERRY CUSTARD

1 1-pound can unsweetened crushed pineapple
1 tablespoon vanilla extract
4 packets Sweet 'N Low
3 cups buttermilk
2 packets unflavored gelatin
1 cup cold water
  fresh or frozen blueberries

In a blender, combine ½ can pineapple with vanilla and
Sweet 'N Low. Slowly add buttermilk and blend a few minutes
longer.

Dissolve gelatin in cold water. Heat slowly until gelatin is clear, then add this to mixture in blender. Blend for 2 minutes.

Pour remaining pineapple into large bowl. Add blended mixture and stir lightly. Pour into dessert dishes, chill and garnish with blueberries.

You may improve the flavor of this dessert by adding almond extract or nutmeg. It will keep for 2 to 3 weeks in the refrigerator.

ANGELO OF MULBERRY STREET

146 MULBERRY STREET (NEAR GRAND)
NEW YORK CITY
966-1277 AND 226-8527

These three dishes from Angelo's are excellent examples of the professional Neapolitan cooking for which the restaurant is known. Owners Gino Silvestri and Johnny Aprea are both from southern Italy, and their constant watch on the kitchen assures patrons of high-quality, authentic cuisine. The restaurant is decorated in classic Italian red-and-gold elegance.

The Fish Platter below is a specialty of the house, easily prepared at home and quite delicious. The Meatballs Neapolitan and Linguine Genovese are surprisingly delicate and interestingly flavored low-priced standards.

FISH PLATTER (SERVES 2 TO 4)

1	1½-pound Maine lobster
¼	cup olive oil
5	cloves garlic, minced
1	12-ounce can Italian plum tomatoes (imported)
	red pepper
	chopped fresh parsley
	chopped fresh basil
	salt
10	clams
6	large shrimps, shelled and deveined
2	dozen mussels

2 cloves garlic, minced
1 cup water

Clean lobster and cut into 4 parts. Sauté in olive oil until meat is tender. Remove from oil.

Add minced 5 cloves of garlic to oil and sauté until lightly browned. Add tomatoes and liquid, breaking tomatoes with your hand. Season with red pepper, parsley, basil and salt. Simmer, uncovered, for ½ hour.

In large pot, place clams, shrimp, mussels, minced 2 cloves of garlic, parsley, basil, red pepper, salt and water. Cover and heat over high flame until mussels and clams are opened. Now add tomato sauce and simmer another 10 minutes.

To serve, place lobster on bottom of platter. Cover with shell-fish and sauce.

MEATBALLS NEAPOLITAN (SERVES 2 TO 4)

1 loaf Italian bread (just the inside dough without the crust)
  milk
1 pound chopped beef
2 cloves garlic, minced
1 tablespoon chopped parsley
  salt
  pepper
4 eggs, separated
  vegetable oil

Soak bread briefly in milk. Squeeze out as much milk as possible and break bread into small pieces. Combine beef, bread, garlic, parsley, salt, pepper and egg yolks, mixing well with your hands. Form balls and dip each ball into unbeaten egg whites.

Deep-fry or pan-fry meatballs in vegetable oil until well browned on all sides.

RAGOUT SAUCE (FOR MEATBALLS)

1 cup olive oil
2 large onions, chopped
2 or 3 cloves garlic, minced
½ pound spareribs (separate ribs)
½ pound beef (any cut), in small pieces
1 12-ounce can Italian plum tomatoes (imported)
½ cup white wine
  salt
  pepper
¼ cup chopped fresh parsley
2 tablespoons chopped fresh basil
1 small can tomato paste

Heat oil and brown onions, garlic and meat. Add tomatoes, wine, salt, pepper, parsley and basil. Cover and simmer gently for 1 hour, stirring occasionally.

Add tomato paste and simmer another ½ hour. Pour over meatballs and serve with pasta.

LINGUINE GENOVESE (4 SERVINGS)

½ cup olive oil
½ pound butter
1½ pounds onions, chopped
3 carrots, chopped
2 or 3 stalks celery, chopped

2 tablespoons chopped parsley
salt
pepper
2 pounds veal shank, cut into pieces
1 cup white wine
2 Italian plum tomatoes

1 pound linguine
2 tablespoons butter
2 tablespoons Parmesan cheese

Very slowly heat olive oil and butter. Add onions, carrots, celery, parsley, salt, pepper and veal. Cover and stew gently for 45 minutes. Add wine, and after 15 minutes mash tomatoes into sauce. Cook another ½ hour, or until veal is tender. (Total cooking time 1½ hours.)

Boil linguine until just done, and drain. Return to pot. Add about 2 tablespoons of sauce, 2 tablespoons butter and Parmesan cheese. Mix well and heat briefly. Serve and cover with remainder of sauce.

ASIA DE CUBA

190 EIGHTH AVENUE
NEW YORK CITY
243-9322

Diagonally across the street from the Elgin Theater, Asia de Cuba is a film-and-food freak's paradise. The line and the wait are usually long (especially after a movie lets out), but the reward is great beans, good meat and superb fried bananas. This is accompanied by loud talk (in various dialects of English, Spanish and Chinese) and lots of action all around you in the small, perpetually crowded, invariably lively room. Owner Mario Perez gladly shared four recipes with us, all excellently prepared by his Spanish-speaking Chinese Cuban chef.

The black bean recipe is an authentic Cuban treatment of the almost universal Latin American staple, prepared one way by Mexicans, another by Brazilians and still another by Dominicans. Even among the Chinese Cuban restaurants in New York there's tremendous variations in black bean quality and flavor. Asia de Cuba's version is excellent, heaped over your favorite rice and spooned up with hearty abandon. (The same recipe may also be successfully applied to kidney beans.)

ROPA VIEJA ("OLD CLOTHES"—SHREDDED BEEF)
(SERVES 4 TO 6)

3 pounds beef flank
2 green peppers, sliced
2 cloves garlic, minced
2 onions, sliced

3 tablespoons olive oil
½ can tomato paste

Boil beef until tender (2 to 3 hours). Drain and reserve stock. Shred beef into short stringlike pieces, removing all fat. To shred, use either two forks or your fingers. Fingers are best once the beef has cooled.

Sauté peppers, garlic and onions in olive oil until onions are golden. Add beef and brown well. Add tomato paste and ½ cup beef stock, stir well, cover and cook over medium heat for 15 to 20 minutes. Remove cover and cook another 5 or 10 minutes over high heat, stirring constantly. When meat is browned and sauce is reduced, serve with rice.

DEVILED SHRIMP (SERVES 2 TO 4)

1 pound large shrimp
1 green pepper, in large pieces
1 onion, thickly sliced
1 clove garlic, minced
2 tablespoons olive oil
1 cup tomato sauce
  Red Devil sauce
  salt
  pepper

Wash and peel shrimp. Devein and butterfly. Boil briefly in water and drain.

Sauté pepper, onion and garlic in olive oil until onions are golden. Add shrimp, tomato sauce and Red Devil to taste. Season with salt and pepper, and simmer uncovered 10 to 15 minutes.

BLACK BEANS (SERVES 4 TO 6)

1 tablespoon olive oil
¼ pound diced salt pork
3 cloves garlic, minced
1 green pepper, chopped fine
1 pound black beans
¼ pound chorizos, diced
  salt
  pepper

Soak beans overnight.

In large, heavy pot, heat oil and sauté pork, garlic and green pepper. Drain the fat. Add beans, chorizos and water 5 times as deep as beans. Simmer, covered, for 4 hours. Remove cover and simmer another hour, until beans are very tender. Season with salt and pepper to taste.

FRIED BANANAS

very ripe bananas
oil for deep frying

Cut bananas on the diagonal into slices 1 inch thick. Drop into very hot oil (400°) and fry until golden (5 minutes or less). Serve hot.

ATLANTIC HOUSE

144 ATLANTIC AVENUE
BROOKLYN
625-7888

Mohammed Almontaser, owner and chef of Atlantic House, is a veteran of a 10-year stint with Restaurant Associates. He has worked at such high spots as the Four Seasons, the Brasserie and La Fonda del Sol. At Atlantic House, he emphasizes his native Yemenite food, although skillfully prepared Continental specialties are also featured.

We highly recommend the kibbe recipe below. Kibbe, though it may sound and taste exotic, is simply Middle Eastern meat loaf. Instead of beef, there's lamb; bulgur takes the place of bread crumbs, and a slightly different range of spices provides the Oriental touch. There are as many variations on kibbe as there are on meat loaf, so feel free to improvise. You will need a meat grinder—for the vegetables—when preparing Mr. Almontaser's kibbe. It's rewarding, but not necessary, to home grind the lamb as well. If you do, be sure to include a healthy amount of fat to keep the kibbe moist.

KIBBE (SERVES 12)

- 5 pounds leg of lamb, ground fine
- ½ pound fine bulgur, rinsed in cold water
- 3 large onions, ground
- 1 green pepper, ground
- 1 bunch parsley, ground

1 tablespoon salt
½ teaspoon pepper
2 teaspoons cumin
2 tablespoons oregano
¾ cup pignola nuts

Combine all ingredients except pignolas. Mix well and adjust seasoning to taste. Press one half of the mixture into a 9×13-inch baking dish. Cover with nuts, then add remaining meat mixture. Press firmly into dish. Bake for 30 minutes at 350°. Cut into diamonds and serve.

STUFFED GRAPE LEAVES (SERVES 12)

5 pounds ground lamb
3 onions, ground
1 bunch parsley, ground
1 green pepper, ground
½ pound rice
2 or more tablespoons oregano
2 or more teaspoons cumin
1 tablespoon salt
½ teaspoon pepper
3 pounds grape leaves
  lamb bones
  stock or water
1 lemon, quartered
1 whole garlic

Combine lamb, onions, pepper, parsley, rice and seasonings. Roll 2 tablespoons of meat mixture in each grape leaf.

Place bones at bottom of pot and lay filled grape leaves over them. Cover with stock. Add lemon quarters and several peeled cloves of garlic. Put a plate over the grape leaves and weight with stones. Cover and simmer for 1 hour or more, until rice and meat are cooked.

BAKLAVA

1 pound sugar
1 tablespoon lemon juice
1 cup water
2 pounds butter and shortening, melted
1 pound filo
1 pound shelled pistachios, chopped

Simmer sugar, lemon juice and water until syrup is thick (about 30 minutes). Let cool.

Brush 9×13-inch (or larger) baking pan with butter-and-shortening mixture. Lay half of the filo in the pan. Pour half the butter mixture over this. Spread pistachios, cover with filo and pour remaining butter over this.

Carefully cut baklava into diamonds and bake at 350° for ½ hour, until filo is golden. Pour cool sugar syrup over hot baklava and serve.

ATRAN CULTURAL CENTER RESTAURANT

25 EAST 78TH STREET
NEW YORK CITY
LE 5-3700

Walking down the stairs into Atran's basement cafeteria, one is immediately greeted by the satisfying aroma of home cooking. Once in the dimly lit, faded yellow room, one is welcomed even more warmly by Helen Henig or Frances Sperber, bending over their small stove and serving deliciously simple, basically Jewish, wonderfully soulful hot food.

The stuffed cabbage explicated below is Mrs. Henig's own version of the ubiquitous dish—a surprisingly sweet and delicate rendition of that often drearily heavy Bar Mitzvah staple. Mrs. Henig, who says she knew nothing about food when she began cooking at Atran over 20 years ago, also developed the recipe for the vegetable soup given here. "The flavor comes just from the vegetables," she notes proudly. It is an excellent soup.

STUFFED CABBAGE (SERVES 4 TO 6)

 ½ cup rice
 1 onion, chopped
 2 tablespoons vegetable oil
1½ pounds lean ground chuck
 1 egg
 2 tablespoons ketchup
 1 teaspoon sugar
   salt

Helen Henig and Frances Sperber, displaying their wares in Atran's basement kitchen.

pepper
1 medium green cabbage

SAUCE

16 ounces tomato purée
 1 apple, sliced
 8 prunes, pitted
 1 onion, sliced
1½ cups water
 1 to 2 teaspoons sugar
   salt and pepper to taste

Boil the rice for about 10 minutes and drain.

Sauté onion in oil just until golden.

In a large bowl, combine the meat, onion, rice, egg, ketchup and sugar. Use your hands to mix well. (Mrs. Henig insists that this is essential.) Add salt and pepper to taste.

With a long, thin knife, cut deeply around the core of the cabbage and remove as much of it as you can. Wash the cabbage and place in some boiling water. As the outer leaves blanch and get soft, remove the cabbage from the water and carefully peel the leaves, returning cabbage to the water until the next layer becomes flexible. Continue this slow process until the cabbage has been completely dismantled. Be patient; try not to burn your fingers. Then slice along the thick rib that runs through the middle of each leaf and remove as much of it as you can without damaging the leaf.

Place about 2 heaping tablespoons of the meat mixture in the center of each leaf. Fold the two sides over it. Flatten; then, starting from the base, roll the leaf tight. There should be no meat sticking out, and the rolled leaf should be fairly firm. Arrange in rows in a baking dish.

Combine ingredients for sauce. Pour over stuffed cabbage leaves. Cover baking dish with aluminum foil and bake at 300° for 1½ to 2 hours, until meat is well done.

Any leftover meat mixture may be made into a meat loaf. Just shape and bake.

VEGETABLE SOUP (SERVES 8 TO 10)

10 cups water
½ cup Scotch barley
½ cup green split peas
½ cup dried lima beans
 3 carrots
 1 parsnip
 1 sweet potato
 1 green pepper
 3 stalks celery
 1 turnip
 1 cup string beans, in 1-inch pieces
 1 tablespoon salt
    handful of fresh chopped dill
 1 to 2 ounces butter or margarine

Bring water to a boil. Add barley, split peas and lima beans, and simmer, covered, for 1 hour.

Cut all vegetables into ½ to 1 inch cubes. Add to soup, salt to taste and simmer another 45 minutes.

Just before serving, stir in the fresh dill and some butter or margarine, if you like. Simmer a few minutes longer.

BAYANIHAN

No longer in operation, Bayanihan was for a short time a good-quality Philippine restaurant. Established by a group of young lawyers and doctors, the restaurant was under the direction of Leonardo Nabayan, who wanted Bayanihan to serve as a gathering place for his compatriots. We're sorry that the restaurant did not survive, but happy to have retrieved chef Loreto Vargas' instructions for the traditional Pork Adobo and the Spanish-influenced Morcón.

PORK ADOBO (SERVES 4 TO 6)

3 pounds pork shoulder or butt
5 whole cloves garlic
½ cup wine vinegar
1 teaspoon ground black pepper
4 teaspoons salt or soy sauce
2 cups water
1 tablespoon lard

Cut pork into pieces about 2 inches wide, 3 inches long and 1½ inches thick. Peel garlic cloves and mash.

Place pork in saucepan. Add vinegar, garlic, pepper, salt or soy sauce and water. Cover and simmer gently until meat is tender and only ¼ cup of liquid remains.

Drain the meat and conserve the broth. Separate the pork from the garlic. Melt the lard in a skillet and fry garlic cloves until brown. Add pork and fry until brown. Add broth and simmer for five minutes before serving.

MORCÓN (SERVES 4 TO 6)

3 pounds beef (top or bottom round)
2 cloves garlic
10 peppercorns
¼ cup vinegar
2 hard-boiled eggs
2 slices ham
2 sausages (Bilbao or Vienna)
¼ pound pork fat
12 olives
  fat for deep frying
2 cups water
½ bay leaf
3 tomatoes, cut into quarters
1 onion, diced
1 tablespoon salt
1 cup tomato sauce

Cut the beef into two slices about 12×16 inches and ½ inch thick. (To do this, slice back and forth through the roast, separating the meat into two interlocked pieces. Pound to flatten.)

In a mortar, pound garlic and peppercorns. Add vinegar and mix well. Marinate meat in this mixture for 15 minutes. Conserve marinade.

Cut eggs in half lengthwise. Cut ham, sausages and pork fat into long strips about ¼ inch wide. Chop olives. Spread beef on a board. Arrange pieces of ham, fat and sausage in alternate rows. Sprinkle with olives. Place egg halves along near edge of beef. Now roll beef tight around the eggs. Sew closed, and tie up ends. Fry each roll in deep fat until browned.

Place beef rolls in saucepan. Add water, bay leaf, tomatoes, onion, salt and the marinade. Cover and simmer until meat is tender. Add tomato sauce and simmer another 5 minutes. Remove rolls and cut into slices. Arrange on platter and pour sauce over meat.

BELCREP

47 WEST 44TH STREET
NEW YORK CITY
986-6678

John Hendrickx began his restaurant career at the 1958 Expo in Brussels, where he ran a small snack bar featuring "pommes frites." He did an excellent business—slicing and frying up to 5,000 pounds of potatoes on busy days. His attempt to run a similar operation at the last New York World's Fair, however, was unsuccessful, so he switched to crêpes . . . and now he is serving over 100 variations on this French/Belgian specialty at Belcrep. Try the Blue Cheese and Apple Filling below, or create your own.

ENDIVES IN HAM (SERVES 2)

4 large Belgian endives
8 thin slices ham
1 cup white sauce
½ cup grated Parmesan cheese

Boil endives in water to cover just until tender (about 15 minutes). Drain.

Roll each endive in 2 slices of ham. Place in a baking dish and cover with white sauce. Sprinkle with Parmesan and place in 350° oven until top is browned.

VEAL STEW (SERVES 4)

4 tablespoons butter
2 pounds veal shoulder, cubed
2 to 3 cups water
2 teaspoons salt
½ teaspoon black pepper
2 tablespoons tarragon
2 medium onions, sliced (or 1 cup dehydrated onions)
½ teaspoon MSG
2 tablespoons cornstarch

Melt butter in a skillet and sear veal over medium heat until light brown on all sides.

In a large pot, combine water, salt, pepper, tarragon and onions. Add veal, bring to a boil, cover and simmer gently for 2 hours, or until veal is tender.

Add MSG and simmer a few minutes longer. Dissolve cornstarch in ¼ cup cold water and add to the stew, stirring until liquid is thickened and translucent.

CRÊPES WITH BLUE CHEESE AND APPLE FILLING (SERVES 4)

4 large apples, peeled and sliced thin
4 tablespoons sugar
1 large egg
1 cup milk

2 cups white flour
½ teaspoon salt
¼ teaspon pepper
  melted butter
½ pound blue cheese mixed with ¼ pound butter

Boil apples in water to cover just until tender. Drain and mix in sugar.

Beat egg with milk. Add flour, salt and pepper, and beat well.

Heat 10-inch skillet and rub with melted butter. Pour in a quarter of the batter and cook over medium-high heat for 1 minute, until crêpe is set. Turn crêpe over and brown on other side. While crêpe is cooking on second side, spread a quarter of the blue cheese mixture over it.

Spread a quarter of the apple mixture on crêpe. Fold edges over to create a square and tap crêpe out onto a plate. Repeat until you have 4 filled crêpes.

THE BELMORE CAFETERIA

407 PARK AVENUE SOUTH
NEW YORK CITY
LE 2-0510

*Open since 1927, the Belmore is today among the last of the
large cafeterias. From the looks of it, it should be here at least
another 50 years. Owners Noel and Myron Siegel are enterprising businessmen, carrying on the work initiated by their father
and his brothers. Even though prices are up, the Belmore continues to serve four to five thousand people daily, with a large part
of the trade consisting of lounging cabbies.*

*Cafeteria fare, prepared in large quantities and exposed to
the hazards of the steam table, is not known for its delicacy. It
can, however, be quite satisfying and is often surprisingly tasty.
The Belmore's Brisket of Beef is an excellent example of cafeteria cuisine at its best; the French Toast is memorable; the
Cheesecake is of the rich, sticks-to-the-roof-of-your-mouth variety.*

BRISKET OF BEEF

2 quarts water
1 large onion, diced
2 stalks celery, diced
1 green pepper, diced
1 No. 2 can tomatoes (1 pound 4 ounces)
  salt
  pepper
5 pounds brisket
2 tablespoons flour

2 tablespoons cornstarch
Gravy Master

Heat oven to 400°. Place water, onions, celery and pepper in large roasting pan. Break up tomatoes and add to the pan. Add salt and pepper to taste. Cover and place in oven. When liquid comes to a boil, add brisket, fat side down. Cover. Reduce heat to 350°. Bake brisket for 1½ hours. Turn over and bake another 1½ hours. Remove beef from liquid and prepare gravy, using flour, cornstarch and Gravy Master. Slice brisket on the diagonal, against the grain, and serve with gravy.

FRENCH TOAST

1 quart milk
3 eggs
¼ cup maple syrup
1 loaf white bread, thickly sliced; should be at least one day old
3 eggs, beaten
  cinnamon

Beat milk, 3 eggs and maple syrup. Soak bread in this mixture until it is very soft. Now dip slices of bread in beaten egg, sprinkle with cinnamon and fry on lightly greased griddle until golden brown.

CHEESECAKE (1 10-INCH CAKE)

4 pounds cream cheese, at room temperature
1 pound sugar
8 eggs

½ cup heavy cream
½ teaspoon vanilla extract
½ to 1 teaspoon grated lemon rind

Blend cheese and sugar thoroughly. Slowly beat in 1 egg at a time, making sure that each egg is thoroughly absorbed before you add the next one. Beat in cream, vanilla and lemon rind. Pour mixture into 10-inch cake mold lined with graham cracker crust or dough (see below).

Bake cake at 450° for 15 minutes, or just until it begins to color at the edges. Remove from oven and let cool for half an hour. Return to 250° oven and bake for 2½ hours, until cake is set. Remove from oven and let cool thoroughly before slicing. Cheesecake tastes best when it is several days old.

DOUGH FOR CHEESECAKE

½ cup sugar
½ pound shortening
1 egg
3 cups sifted flour
1¾ tablespoons dry whole-milk solids
1 teaspoon salt

Blend sugar and shortening until creamy. Beat in egg, flour, milk solids and salt. Chill for 1 hour before rolling. Roll out to about ¼-inch thickness. Place over bottom of cake mold and cut to fit. Grease mold lightly and place dough in bottom. Bake for 5 to 10 minutes. Remove from oven. Roll out dough to line sides of mold. Press in firmly. Now pour in cheesecake mixture and bake as above.

THE BRAZILIAN COFFEE RESTAURANT

45 WEST 46TH STREET
NEW YORK CITY
265-9711

The Brazilian Coffee Restaurant has the distinction of having been the first Brazilian/Portuguese restaurant in the United States. Since its opening in 1962, it has moved through various related hands and two addresses; it is currently owned by Francelina and Valentim Oliveira. Francelina, a small, intense woman with remarkably expressive eyes, is responsible for the high-quality cooking. Her facility in the kitchen is no mere acquired skill. It seems to have been absorbed fully by her body, which knows instinctively all the subtle movements and rhythms required by her creations. Cooking is her dance, and it is a beautiful one.

Valentim is responsible for the business end of the restaurant, and he handles these affairs with the same ease his wife exercises in the kitchen. Together they are an outstanding team running a pleasant and personal restaurant.

SHRIMP À BAIANA (SERVES 4 TO 6)

1 pound shrimp
4 medium tomatoes, cut into eighths
3 onions, in thick slices
4 green peppers, in eighths

½ cup tomato sauce
4 tablespoons beer
2 tablespoons olive oil

Clean shrimp and butterfly, or make a few diagonal slits across each back.

Place all ingredients in a large pot. Cover and stew gently for 15 minutes, occasionally shaking pot to prevent sticking. Add water if desired.

BACALÃO GOMEZ DE SA (SERVES 4)

1½ pounds salt cod
1 pound potatoes, peeled
½ pound onions, chopped
   olive oil
4 cloves garlic, minced
   salt
   black pepper
2 onions, sliced
   handful fresh chopped parsley
2 hard boiled eggs, chopped
   olives, chopped

Soak cod in cold water for 48 hours, changing water once or twice. Drain, rinse and place in pot. Cover with water and bring to a boil. Simmer, covered, for 15 to 20 minutes. Drain and pick out bones.

Boil potatoes until soft. Cut into ½-inch cubes.

Sauté chopped onions in olive oil until golden. Mix half with the codfish, half with the potatoes. Sauté garlic and again add half to the potatoes, half to the cod. Season potato mixture with salt and pepper.

Place codfish in bottom of baking dish. Cover with sliced onions, then with potato mixture. Sprinkle with parsley. Cover with foil and bake at 350° for 15 minutes. Garnish with chopped eggs and olives.

CHICKEN BOSSA NOVA

olive oil
minced garlic
chicken pieces
salt
pepper

Deep-fry chicken in olive oil, to which some garlic has been added. Drain, season with salt and pepper, and serve topped with sautéed garlic.

PUDÍM DI CARAMELO (SERVES 6 TO 8)

1 cup sugar
2 tablespoons water
6 eggs
2 cups milk
1 7-ounce can sweetened condensed milk
3 tablespoons sugar

Heat 1 cup sugar with water until sugar melts. Continue to heat over a medium flame until sugar syrup begins to turn brown. Stir syrup and remove from heat.

Quickly beat remaining ingredients. Pour caramel syrup into baking dish and add custard mixture. Place dish in a pan of water and bake at 350° until custard is set (about 40 minutes).

Joaquim Gonzalez, the Brazilian Pavilion's debonair proprietor—and former soccer player— strikes a pose beside his cash register.

BRAZILIAN PAVILION

141 EAST 52ND STREET
NEW YORK CITY
758-8129

Joaquim Gonzalez, the capable and congenial proprietor of the Brazilian Pavilion, generously offered to share half a dozen recipes with us when we first approached him. Much to his own surprise and chagrin, though, he and his chef were stumped when it came to breaking down proportions and specifying procedures. Working together, however, we were able to reconstruct the following three dishes: Churrasco Gaucho, a tangy Brazilian steak; Caldeirada de Peixe, a superb Portuguese fish stew, and Coconut Custard, a very *sweet dessert.*

The Brazilian Pavilion is Mr. Gonzalez' second restaurant, and it successfully incorporates all the knowledge he acquired during his 10 "apprentice" years in the New York restaurant business. (Like so many others, Mr. Gonzalez spent much of that time working for Restaurant Associates.) The design of the Pavilion is clean and precise, enlivened by the bright Brazilian colors (yellow, green, blue) which are used throughout. The staff works smoothly and efficiently, though the professional order never masks the spontaneous warmth radiated by Mr. Gonzalez and his employees. Brazilian food seems designed to make its eaters (and servers) happy.

CHURRASCO GAUCHO (SERVES 4)

¼ cup vinegar
¼ cup oil
1 onion, chopped fine
2 tomatoes, chopped fine
½ teaspoon salt
   drop Tabasco
2 pounds top sirloin, sliced into 4 rectanguiar steaks

   Combine vinegar, oil, onions, tomatoes and seasoning to form a marinade. Marinate steaks in this mixture for 45 minutes. Broil and serve.

CALDEIRADA DE PEIXE (SERVES 8)

1 pound salt cod
18 clams
3 pounds striped bass
2 pounds whiting
1 pound shrimp
2 pounds squid

1 onion, diced
2 tomatoes, diced
2 green peppers, diced
½ cup vegetable oil
1 cup tomato sauce
½ cup white wine

3 bay leaves
   salt
   pepper
3 pounds potatoes, diced
2 tomatoes, sliced
1 onion, sliced
1 green pepper, sliced
½ cup tomato sauce

Soak cod for 48 hours and rinse. Boil clams and remove from shells. Remove heads and tails from fish, then cut into chunks. Clean shrimp. Cut squid into 1-inch lengths.

Sauté diced onions, tomatoes, and peppers in oil until onions are golden. Add shrimp, clams, squid and water to cover. Cover pot and simmer for 15 minutes. Add bass, whiting, 1 cup tomato sauce, wine and bay leaves. Season with salt and pepper. Simmer another 8 to 10 minutes.

In a separate pot, place potatoes, sliced tomatoes, sliced onion and sliced pepper, plus cod and ½ cup tomato sauce. Add water so that liquid is about ¾ as deep as the vegetables and fish. Cover and simmer for 20 minutes until potatoes are tender. Remove cod from this mixture and discard. Add remainder to the fish stew, mix well and simmer together for 5 minutes.

COCONUT CUSTARD (SERVES 4)

2 4-ounce cans Baker's "Southern Style" coconut
3 cups boiling water
7 to 8 tablespoons sugar
½ cup water
3 beaten egg yolks

Add coconut to boiling water. Simmer, uncovered, for 45 to 60 minutes, until coconut is soft and most of the liquid is evaporated.

Heat sugar and ½ cup water over high flame until mixture is light brown (about 10 minutes). Add this to the coconut and mix well. Let cool.

Add egg yolks to coconut. Mix well and refrigerate. Serve with slices of fresh white cheese.

CABANA CARIOCA

123 WEST 45TH STREET
NEW YORK CITY
582-8510

Upstairs on 45th Street at Cabana Carioca, you can sit by a window and watch the busy street action below, or you can focus your attention on the food served in huge quantities and accompanied by generous good cheer from the management. The Brazilian atmosphere is thick here—a short visit to the back-room counter should convince you of the restaurant's authenticity.

The chef kindly gave us his recipe for Feijoada Completa, the Brazilian national dish and a Wednesday and Saturday special at Cabana Carioca. Best made in huge quantities to feed a tired, hungry extended family, it is traditionally served as the midday meal on Saturdays. After sating themselves on beans, meat, rice, collards, oranges and mandioca flour, the various members of the family are generally ready for a good sound sleep. The beer which ordinarily accompanies the meal adds to the satisfied stupor. Preparing feijoada at home in America is a pointed reminder of our isolated way of life—there's no way to make the dish for two, and you'll probably wish there were more of you to enjoy this totally satisfying meal. If you have a big enough pot, and enough friends, try making it for 16 rather than 8.

FEIJOADA COMPLETA (SERVES 8)

1 pound black beans
½ pound dried beef (carne seca)
½ pound smoked ribs
¼ pound cow's tongue
    assorted pig's feet, tail, ears (4 pieces in all)
4 bay leaves
1 onion, chopped
2 cloves garlic, minced
    olive oil
1 teaspoon salt
2 to 4 chorizos (Portuguese type)
2 pounds collard greens
4 oranges
3 cups rice
    hot pepper sauce
    mandioca flour

The night before you plan to serve the dish, wash the beans well and cover with water. The best way to prepare the feijoada is in an 8- or 10-quart pot; the water should reach the 6-quart mark. Also the night before, cut dried beef into 8 pieces, wash well and cover with water. The meat needs a thorough soaking to extract all the salt used in preserving it. Soaking also facilitates the removal of the orange wax coating.

Drain beef and add to beans, with ribs, tongue, pig pieces and bay leaves. Cover, bring to a boil and simmer 1½ hours.

Fry onion and garlic in 2 tablespoons olive oil. Add salt, and add this mixture to the beans. At this time also add chorizos. Let simmer at least another hour, until the beans are soft and the liquid is thickened.

To make the feijoada "completa," wash the collards and chop fine. Heat about ½ cup olive oil in large pot, add the greens, cover and stew over low heat for about 20 minutes. Peel the oranges and cut into eighths. Prepare the rice.

To serve, remove meat from the beans. Cut so you have 8 pieces of each type. Place one piece of each type of meat on each plate. Ladle beans over the meat and arrange rice, greens and orange sections on each plate. At table, have handy some hot pepper sauce and a bowl of mandioca flour to sprinkle over the beans and cut the spiciness of the hot sauce.

DOCE DE LEITE

1 can Carnation sweetened condensed milk

This may be the easiest noninstant dessert you can make. It is a traditional Brazilian favorite, a creamy caramel sweet prepared with a great deal of time and care. Cabana Carioca's version, however, is so simple that you are likely to feel guilty—getting so much reward for so little work. Americo, the restaurant's happy owner, laughed wickedly as he recited the recipe. "First, you have to take the labels off the can. Then you put it in water and boil it!" We didn't quite understand at first, but he insisted that that was all there was to it: take labels off can, immerse in water, boil for 2½ hours, cool, open and serve cold. Doce de Leite is almost unbearably sweet and caloric, so serve in thin slices, along with slices of fresh white cheese (queijo blanco) and strong espresso.

CAFE MANILA

248 EAST 52ND STREET
NEW YORK CITY
753-6987

Cafe Manila is a quiet, unpretentious restaurant/cafeteria serving authentic Philippine food. The Philippine style is an amalgam of Chinese, Spanish, Portuguese and native island cooking, resulting in a distinctive cuisine with familiar overtones. There is a heavy use of vinegar, as in the Chicken Adobo, the national dish. Nelly Del Rosario, who with her husband owns and manages Cafe Manila, insists that it can never taste as good in America as it does in the Philippines, where chicken is more abundant, more tender and more flavorful than it is here. Nevertheless, we recommend the dish as an interesting and cheap chicken variation.

CHICKEN ADOBO

- 1 3-pound frying chicken
  salt
  pepper
- ½ cup vinegar
- 2 cups water
- 2 tablespoons soy sauce
- 1 clove garlic, minced
- ½ bay leaf
- 2 tablespoons vegetable oil

Clean chicken and cut into serving pieces. Season with salt and pepper and let stand for 10 or 15 minutes. Place in pot with vinegar and water and add all seasonings. Cover and simmer gently until chicken is tender and liquid is almost all evaporated (about 30 minutes). Add oil and fry over high heat until chicken is browned.

LUMPIA FRITO (MAKES 6 DOZEN SMALL DUMPLINGS)

1 pound ground pork butt
1 pound ground beef
1 cup chopped water chestnuts
1 cup chopped bamboo shoots
½ cup finely chopped onions
3 egg yolks
  soy sauce
  salt
  pepper
1 package egg roll wrappers
1 or 2 eggs, beaten
  vegetable oil for deep frying

Combine pork, beef, water chestnuts, bamboo shoots, onions and egg yolks. Season with soy sauce, salt and pepper to taste. Mix well.

Cut each egg roll wrapper in half. Place filling in a strip along the center and roll to form a long narrow dumpling. Seal with beaten egg. Deep-fry in hot oil until golden. Drain. Cut each dumpling into 3 segments. Serve with Sweet and Sour Sauce.

SWEET AND SOUR SAUCE

½ cup vinegar
2 tablespoons soy sauce
1 cup water
1 cup sugar
1 teaspoon salt
1 tablespoon ketchup
  dash pepper
1 tablespoon cornstarch dissolved in ¼ cup water

Mix vinegar, soy, sugar, water, salt, ketchup and pepper in a saucepan and bring to a boil. Add cornstarch and stir in well. Simmer a few minutes, stirring constantly. Let cool, chill and serve.

CAFFE DA ALFREDO

17 PERRY STREET
NEW YORK CITY
989-7028

Alfredo Viazzi is the founder of three high-quality Italian restaurants which bear his name—the Caffe, Trattoria and Tavola Calda da Alfredo. All are located in the West Village.

A handsome and vibrant man, Mr. Viazzi has been in and out of the restaurant business—here and in Italy—for 20 years. He has a sure sense of how to run a successful restaurant, and he loves his work. His standards are high, his ingredients fresh, his preparations imaginative and tasty.

At the Caffe, one may sample any of the dishes below, plus an array of Roman sandwiches, antipasti and nonalcoholic beverages. The atmosphere is relaxed, the style elegant.

SPAGHETTINI CARBONARA (SERVES FOUR)

¼ pound pancetta
1 stick butter
½ tablespoon white wine
1 pound spaghettini
½ pint heavy cream
2 egg yolks, lightly beaten
1 cup grated Parmesan cheese
freshly ground black pepper

In a medium saucepan, sauté pancetta (whole slices or julienned). Add small lump of butter to pan. As pancetta starts to become crisp, add the white wine. Continue to cook until pancetta is completely cooked and aroma of wine is gone. Drain.

Cook spaghettini in 2 gallons of boiling salted water (5 to 7 minutes after water comes to second boil). Drain.

In a large sauté pan, melt remainder of butter over medium heat. Add spaghettini and mix thoroughly. Slowly add cream, then egg yolks, mixing well and being careful not to let the eggs curdle. Add pancetta to mixture. Quickly add half of the grated Parmesan; then grind some fresh black pepper over the whole and mix well again. Serve. (Note: This entire process must be accomplished quickly.)

At the table, add remainder of cheese atop spaghettini, plus more pepper if desired. The name "carbonara" means "coal man's style"—hence the black specks of pepper.

RIGATONI ALLA VIAREGGINA (SERVES 4)

¼ cup olive oil
⅓ teaspoon finely chopped garlic
   pinch of oregano
   pinch of thyme
   pinch of dried basil
   black pepper
¼ cup finely chopped Italian parsley
 4 anchovy fillets
 1 10-ounce can Italian tuna in olive oil (Genova brand
      preferred)
 1 can (1 pound 14 ounces) Italian peeled tomatoes (Vitelli
      brand preferred)
 1 pound rigatoni macaroni
 1 tablespoon butter
½ cup grated Parmesan cheese

In a deep saucepan, heat olive oil. Add garlic and sauté over low flame. Do not burn. Add all seasonings, including parsley, and anchovies. Mix well until fillets melt thoroughly. Add tuna, breaking it up in the pan with a fork. Add peeled tomatoes, breaking them up with your fingers as you do so, including about half of their packing liquid. Simmer 25 minutes over a medium flame.

Cook rigatoni in 2 gallons of salted water for 10 to 12 minutes after the second boil. Drain.

In a large sauté pan, melt butter and sauté rigatoni. Add enough sauce to coat the pasta. Mix well. Place on a serving platter and pour remainder of sauce over the pasta. Serve with Parmesan cheese.

PAGLIA E FIENO ("STRAW AND HAY") (SERVES 6)

1½ sticks butter
1 clove garlic, chopped fine
1½ pounds sweet Italian sausage (remove casings)
¼ cup chopped Italian parsley
1 teaspoon basil
1 generous pinch tarragon
1 pinch thyme
1 pinch oregano
1 pinch sage
salt
freshly ground black pepper
1½ pounds fresh mushrooms
1 pound fresh green tagliarini
1 pound fresh white tagliarini
½ pint heavy cream
½ cup grated Parmesan cheese

To prepare sauce: In a deep, large skillet, melt one stick of butter. Add garlic and sauté slightly without burning. Add sausage and seasonings. Simmer for 20 minutes, stirring occasionally.

Wash mushrooms thoroughly, slice roughly and dry. Add them to the sauce and cook an additional 15 minutes. Keep hot.

Drop both kinds of tagliarini into a 2-gallon pot of boiling salted water. Simmer for 5 minutes. Drain. In a large sauté pan, melt remainder of butter. Add pasta and sauté lightly over a low flame. Add half of the sauce and all of the cream. Mix well until cream thickens. This process should not take more than 3 minutes.

Place pasta in serving platter, top with remaining sauce and serve with Parmesan cheese and freshly ground pepper.

CRISP SALAD GREENS WITH HOT ANCHOVY DRESSING AND PECORINO CHEESE (SERVES 6)

1 medium head Boston lettuce
1 medium head romaine lettuce
1 small head escarole
1 small bunch watercress
1 small head chicory
1 cucumber
5 red radishes
4 scallions
¼ cup olive oil
2 teaspoons anchovy paste
  pepper
¼ cup grated Pecorino (Romano) cheese

Wash and cut greens, using only tender white parts. Peel and slice cucumber into thin medallions; trim and slice radishes; julienne scallions. Drain thoroughly and chill in refrigerator.

Heat olive oil over a low flame. Stir in anchovy paste until well blended and add pepper to taste. Remove greens from refrigerator and pour over them 3 tablespoons of your favorite dressing (not French or cheese). Mix well. Sprinkle the Pecorino over salad, then pour on the hot anchovy sauce. Serve.

COLD ZABAGLIONE SAUCE WITH FRESH STRAWBERRIES AND WHIPPED CREAM (SERVES 4)

    2 pints heavy cream
       sugar
    1 pint fresh strawberries
   10 egg yolks
   ⅓ cup sweet sherry

Whip cream, sweeten to taste and store in refrigerator. Clean and wash strawberries, then cool in refrigerator.

Place egg yolks, 1½ tablespoons sugar and sherry in zabaglione pot (round-bottomed copper pot). Break up yolks and mix well. Place pot over boiling water and whip contents briskly at a steady pace until eggs, sugar and sherry become a smooth blend of custard consistency. (This must be done over high heat; be careful not to submerge zabaglione pot too deeply in water.)

Let zabaglione cool. Beat with whipped cream, then chill in refrigerator for ½ hour. Pour over strawberries and serve.

CEDARS OF LEBANON

39 EAST 30TH STREET
NEW YORK CITY
OR 9-6755

Adorned with posters of Middle Eastern cities, along with mock-Oriental rugs, Cedars of Lebanon succeeds in creating a faintly Middle Eastern atmosphere. (Low Arabic music adds to the effect.) Service is professional and pleasant; the food is well prepared and attractively presented.

Middle Eastern cuisine has a range of flavors and textures all its own; related to Greek and Indian cuisine, it is still a world unto itself. The flavors are in some way dark and musky, often enlivened by the sharp tang of lemon juice. Baba Ghanouj exhibits these characteristics. Tabbouleh is a light and refreshing salad, nice to look at and wonderful to taste; it is prepared with bulgur, a wheat product with numerous applications.

BABA GHANOUJ (4 TO 6 SERVINGS)

1 medium eggplant
olive oil
5 teaspoons tahini (sesame paste)
1 to 2 teaspoons lemon juice
1 teaspoon water
¾ teaspoon salt
¼ teaspoon garlic powder

Bake eggplant at 350° for 1½ to 2 hours, until it is quite soft.

Let eggplant cool; then slit skin and scoop out all the pulp. Place in a small bowl. Cover with 1 or 2 tablespoons of olive oil and refrigerate for at least 3 hours.

Remove eggplant from refrigerator and mince well. Add tahini, lemon juice, water, salt and garlic powder. Blend well. Stir in 1 or 2 teaspoons of olive oil and serve cold. One-quarter teaspoon (or more) of cumin may be added for a still stronger Middle Eastern flavor.

TABBOULEH

1 cup fine bulgur
olive oil
1 bunch Italian parsley, chopped very fine
1 bunch scallions, chopped very fine
3 to 4 ripe tomatoes, chopped very fine
1 tablespoon lemon juice
1 teaspoon salt
handful of crushed mint leaves (fresh or dried)

Rinse bulgur and place in bowl. Cover with water as deep again as the grain. Add 2 tablespoons olive oil and let bulgur soak for at least one hour.

Drain bulgur and combine with vegetables. Mix well, using your hands. Add lemon juice, salt, mint leaves and olive oil to taste.

Other fresh chopped vegetables may be added for variety: cucumbers, onions, green pepper.

Brigette Chezelle on Greenwich Avenue—the image of herself, duplicating an earlier photograph with startling precision.

CHEZ BRIGITTE

77 GREENWICH AVENUE
NEW YORK CITY
CH 3-9542

Disguised as a run-of-the-mill luncheonette, Chez Brigitte is in fact an excellent French restaurant. A sign boasts that the restaurant seats 250 people—11 at a time. Space is limited to two back-to-back counters, where you can sit casually, if not comfortably, and rap with other customers or converse in French, English or Spanish with Brigitte, the restaurant's energetic and charming proprietress. A native of Provence, Brigitte ran a small restaurant in Marseille before coming to America. She has been serving her tasty Provençal cooking to appreciative customers here for over 13 years.

"La cuisine de Provence," she notes, "est plus maison"—that is, it's a homier, more robust style than French haute or even bourgeois cuisine. Vegetables in abundance, olive oil, garlic, fresh herbs and numerous varieties of fish bespeak the sunny Mediterranean origins of the style. Vegetables are never boiled or steamed but stewed, with a bit of oil and salt. Fish is always well seasoned, but never enough to mask the original sea flavor, which comes through most notably in Brigitte's superb fish soup. The three recipes Brigitte shared with us are excellent examples of this savory food so different from typical American preparations.

MORUE PROVENÇALE (SERVES 4)

1 to 1½ pounds salt cod
½ cup chopped onions
2 cups chopped fresh tomatoes
2 garlic cloves, crushed
  olive oil
  flour
2 tablespoons chopped parsley
2 sweet pickles, sliced

Soak codfish for 24 to 48 hours. Rinse and drain.

Stew onions, tomatoes and garlic in 2 tablespoons olive oil for 10 minutes.

Dredge fish in flour and brown on both sides in hot oil. Cover with sauce, cover and simmer gently for 10 minutes. Garnish with pickles and parsley. Serve.

RATATOUILLE NIÇOISE (SERVES 6)

2 zucchinis, diced
1 large onion, diced
1 large or two small eggplants, diced
4 fresh tomatoes, diced
4 green peppers, diced
2 potatoes, diced
  (All the vegetables should be in ½-inch cubes. Peel potatoes, but do not remove zucchini or eggplant skins.)

½ cup olive oil
 1 tablespoon oregano
 2 or 3 bay leaves
10 capers
 2 teaspoons salt
½ teaspoon black pepper

Combine all ingredients in a large, heavy casserole and cover. Place in 350° oven for 1 hour, stirring occasionally. Serve. This ratatouille also makes an excellent omelet filling. Just spoon onto an omelet as it begins to set, fold and serve. Note that this ratatouille, unlike most versions, is cooked in the oven, rather than over heat. Cooking in the oven makes for even, slower, less worrisome cooking . . . and results in an outstandingly flavorful stew.

SALADE NIÇOISE (SERVES 4)

4 carrots
4 potatoes, peeled
4 stalks celery, diced
1 tablespoon vinegar
3 tablespoons olive oil
2 cloves garlic, minced
1 teaspoon oregano

Boil carrots and potatoes just until tender. Drain and dice. Chill.

Combine diced carrots, potatoes and celery. Mix remaining ingredients to form a dressing, then pour over vegetables and toss. Serve chilled.

Nawaf Saleh and Jamal Beyrouti with "proofs" of the noted Damascus pita bread.

THE DAMASCUS BAKERY

195 ATLANTIC AVENUE
BROOKLYN
UN 5-1456

When it opened in 1929, The Damascus Bakery was a small family shop on Atlantic Avenue, catering to the neighboring Middle Eastern community. "Chammy," or "Pita" as the Israelis call it, was virtually unknown outside this enclave, and The Damascus was simply a good local bakery. Today, however, this unique bread has acquired a following, and The Damascus is not only supplying numerous New York supermarkets, but also shipping its products as far as California and Texas. The original small bakery on Atlantic Avenue has been supplemented by a fully automated plant at 498 President Street. There, 7,000 loaves of Pita are produced every hour. The bread, which is prepared without sweetening or oil, is light and versatile. It is easy to make and requires little time for either rising or baking. Remember that your oven must be very hot in order for the Pita to bake properly.

PITA

25 to 30 small loaves:

- 5 packages (10 teaspoons) dry yeast or 5 teaspoons fresh yeast
- 2½ tablespoons salt
- 5 cups lukewarm water
- 5 pounds patent flour

5 to 6 small loaves:

1 package (2 teaspoons) dry yeast or 1 teaspoon fresh yeast
½ tablespoon salt
1 cup lukewarm water
1 pound patent flour

Dissolve yeast and salt in lukewarm water. Slowly blend in flour. Turn out onto floured board and knead vigorously for 10 minutes, until dough is smooth. Break into approximately 3-ounce pieces and shape into balls. Arrange balls on a board, cover with a damp cloth and leave in a warm place for ½ hour. Now roll each ball out into a circle about 6 inches in diameter. Proof for another half hour.

Heat oven to the highest possible temperature. (At the Damascus the ovens are set at 700°, but this is usually unattainable at home.) Arrange dough on baking sheets and place in oven for approximately 10 minutes. Bread will puff up in the oven, then collapse when you remove it from the heat. The baking time will vary according to the temperature of your oven; experiment with one loaf to determine the proper timing before baking a whole batch. Bread is ready when it has risen and is lightly browned in spots.

MEAT PIES

PITA DOUGH

For 5 pounds of flour, add ¼ cup vegetable oil to recipe just given for the basic dough.

Divide into 1½-ounce sections and shape into balls. Proof for ½ hour. Roll flat and place a few teaspoons of Meat Filling in center. Fold to form a flat triangle and pinch edges together.

Proof for 15 minutes. Brush with oil and bake at 400° for 10 to 15 minutes.

MEAT FILLING

1 pound ground lamb
¾ cup yogurt
⅜ cup lemon juice
¼ cup pine nuts
¼ cup chopped onion
  salt
  pepper

Combine all ingredients, seasoning to taste with salt and pepper.

SESAME RINGS

Pita Dough
sesame seeds
water

After you have kneaded the dough, shape into several large balls (3 to 5 inches in diameter). Proof for half an hour. Now roll each ball out into a cylinder about 1 inch in diameter. Bring ends of cylinder together to form a circular ring. Dip each ring in water, then dip into sesame seeds, coating well. Proof for ½ hour. Bake at the highest temperature your oven will attain for 5 minutes, until dough has risen and bread is golden brown.

Reflections in the window of East-West. Chef Richard Price smiles out from the lower left. Beside him is proud owner Jimmy Guido.

EAST-WEST COOKERY

105 EAST 9TH STREET
NEW YORK CITY
477-9412

Richard Price, cook and manager of East-West, first got interested in natural foods when a diet of brown rice, miso and adzuki beans cured him of an illness he had been unable to shake using conventional medicines. He decided then to learn about Oriental cooking and landed a job as a dishwasher in a Chinese restaurant. Later he worked as a cook in a bar, preparing steaks, chops and cakes. From there, he went to a natural-foods restaurant and then to a French one. He had always dreamed of having a wok kitchen of his own, which is what he now has at East-West. It is one of the nicest kitchens we have seen, allowing him to work gracefully and with complete control.

Born, like the restaurant, under the sign of Cancer, Richard seems to be a cook by nature. He is deeply interested in his work and brings an inquiring and active mind to bear on his creations. His style is eclectic, constantly evolving. His professed ambition is to use techniques from all types of cooking to create healthful, tasty dishes.

SEVEN GRAIN SPLIT PEA VEGETABLE SOUP
(SERVES 10)

12 cups water
 1 cup bonito flakes
 1 tablespoon olive oil
 2 bay leaves

½ cup cooked brown rice
½ cup cooked bulgur
½ cup cooked corn (off the cob)
½ cup cooked pearl barley
½ cup cooked steel-cut oat flakes
½ cup cooked kasha
½ cup cooked millet
1 cup split peas

3 tablespoons olive or corn oil
2 cups onions, sliced into very thin half-moons
1 teaspoon salt
2 cups very finely minced green pepper
1 cup water or stock
1 cup finely chopped celery
½ cup finely chopped watercress

1 teaspoon onion salt
½ teaspoon garlic salt
¼ teaspoon ginger powder
1 tablespoon basil
½ cup tamari

Bring water to a boil. Add bonito flakes and let water come to second boil. Immediately remove from heat and strain stock to remove fish flakes.

Add 1 tablespoon olive oil, bay leaves and the seven cooked grains to the stock. Bring to a boil and simmer for 10 minutes. Add split peas and continue to simmer until peas have dissolved and soup is thick and creamy.

Heat 3 tablespoons olive or corn oil in large skillet. Add onions and cook over high flame until onions are translucent. Add salt. Reduce heat and allow onions to cook until sweet. Add green peppers and sauté briefly. Add the cup of water or stock, the celery and the watercress. Cover pan and simmer until all liquid is absorbed.

Add vegetables to soup and simmer for 15 minutes.

Add final seasonings to soup and serve.

WELSH ONION SOUP (SERVES 8 TO 10)

 8 cups water
   olive oil
   rosemary
   marjoram
   onion salt
   tamari
   garlic powder
 4 cups bulgur
12 cups water
 1 cup bonito flakes
 6 tablespoons olive or corn oil
 6 cups onions, sliced into very thin half-moons
 2 teaspoons salt
 2 cups very finely minced green pepper
 2 cups very finely minced celery
 2 cups very finely minced leeks
 2 cups cooked white beans

Bring 8 cups water to boil and season with olive oil, rosemary, marjoram, onion salt, tamari and garlic powder. Add bulgur and let liquid come to second boil. Cover and simmer for about 20 minutes, until water is absorbed and bulgur grains are separate.

Bring 12 cups water to boil. Add bonito flakes and bring to second boil. Immediately remove from heat and strain stock to remove fish flakes.

Add cooked bulgur to stock and simmer for 20 minutes.

Heat 6 tablespoons oil in large skillet. Add onions and sauté over high flame until they are soft and translucent. Add salt. Reduce heat and cook until onions are sweet. Add peppers and sauté. Add 2 to 3 cups stock to cooked vegetables; then add celery and leeks. Cover and simmer until all water is absorbed.

Add vegetables to soup and simmer for 20 minutes. Add white beans at end and season with tamari.

FILLET OF SOLE CORDON BLEU (SERVES 6)

   6 good-sized fillets of sole (or flounder)
1½ cups cooked baby shrimp
   2 cups grated Jarlsberg cheese, seasoned with dill, garlic salt
        and rice wine
   2 eggs
   1 cup salted water
   1 cup unbleached white flour
   1 cup bread crumbs, seasoned with salt and garlic powder
        oil for deep frying

Pound each fillet with a meat tenderizer until flexible.

Place a good handful of shrimp and cheese in center of each fillet. Fold fillet over filling and secure with toothpicks.

Beat eggs with water. Dip each fillet into egg mixture, then dredge in flour. Dip again in eggs, then coat with bread crumbs. Cool breaded fish in refrigerator.

Deep-fry in hot oil (375°) for about 7 minutes, until fish is cooked and cheese has melted. Serve with wild rice boiled in salted water with some sesame oil.

JAPANESE FRUIT KANTEN (12 SERVINGS)

4 sticks white agar-agar
2 quarts apple juice
2 quarts grape juice
1 cup raisins
1 cup dried apricots
1 cup dried apples
4 tablespoons vanilla extract
2 tablespoons almond extract
1 tablespoon pumpkin pie spice

Combine all ingredients in large pot. Bring to a boil and simmer for 30 minutes.

Pour into individual dishes or one large refrigerator tray. Let cool. Chill.

TOPPING

1 cup raisins
2 cups apple juice
2 bean curd cakes (tofu)

Boil raisins in apple juice until they are soft and enlarged. Let cool.

Place raisins and juice in blender with tofu. Blend until thick and creamy.

Serve Kanten with as much Topping as your taste can handle.

EPICURE'S KITCHEN CUISINE

470 WEST 23RD STREET
NEW YORK CITY
242-0285

Epicure's Kitchen was originally an outgoing gourmet food service for "convenience-oriented" people who wanted to "enjoy the labors of an international cook at the lowest cost possible." The service expanded into a restaurant, still owned and operated by René Ippoliti and still serving the same quality food at moderate prices. The general style is European eclectic, with French, Italian and German specialties making appearances on the menu. Mr. Ippoliti is a competent and conscientious cook with wide-ranging abilities; he works alone in his well-organized kitchen and continues to prepare most of his dishes to order.

The recipes below are somewhat complex, involving several stages and numerous pots. The key to success is planning, so please read the directions carefully before rolling up your sleeves.

ROLLED EGGPLANT (SERVES 6 TO 8)

1 medium eggplant
1 cup peanut oil
1 cup white flour
3 eggs
1 cup fine bread crumbs
1 pound mozzarella cheese, cut into thin strips
Tomato Sauce (see below)
½ cup grated Parmesan cheese

Wash and peel eggplant. Cut lengthwise in ⅛-inch slices and let stand ½ to 1 hour.

Heat oil in skillet or saucepan. Dredge eggplant in flour, dip in beaten eggs and coat with bread crumbs. Deep-fry in oil (350°) just until golden. Drain on paper towels.

Place 4 or 5 strips of mozzarella on each slice of eggplant, sprinkle with 1 tablespoon Parmesan and roll. Lay rolled eggplant in a baking dish. Cover with Tomato Sauce and sprinkle with remaining Parmesan. Bake 30 minutes in a 350° oven, or until cheese is completely melted. Serve with a salad as a main dish or as a side vegetable.

TOMATO SAUCE

- 2 large onions, chopped
- 3 cloves garlic, minced
- 4 tablespoons oil
- 2 16-ounce cans Italian plum tomatoes (imported)
- 2 tablespoons tomato paste
- 2 bay leaves
- ½ teaspoon thyme
- ½ teaspoon sugar
- ⅛ teaspoon black pepper

Sauté onions and garlic in oil just until they become translucent.

Add tomatoes, tomato paste and seasonings. Stir well and simmer gently, uncovered, for 1½ to 2 hours. Stir occasionally.

Strain sauce through food mill.

CHICKEN ROSEMARY (SERVES 4)

1 onion, diced
1 clove garlic, minced
vegetable oil
2 tablespoons white flour
1 cup white wine
1 cup chicken stock or broth
2 tablespoons tomato pulp (from canned Italian tomatoes)
½ teaspoon rosemary
½ teaspoon thyme
1 bay leaf
⅛ teaspoon black pepper
1 3-pound frying chicken, disjointed
2 green peppers, quartered

In a saucepan, sauté onion and garlic in 2 tablespoons oil until translucent. Add flour and stir well. Cook gently about 10 minutes, stirring constantly, until mixture becomes pasty.

Add wine, chicken stock and tomato pulp. Stir well and bring to a boil. Skim off foam, reduce heat and add seasonings. Simmer gently for 10 minutes.

Dredge chicken in flour and brown lightly in hot oil. Arrange pieces in a casserole and cover with green peppers. Pour sauce over chicken, cover and simmer gently for 30 minutes. Remove peppers and simmer another 10 to 15 minutes. Remove chicken from sauce and reduce sauce rapidly. Pour sauce over chicken and peppers and serve.

FAIRMONT VIENNESE RESTAURANT

1135 AMSTERDAM AVENUE
NEW YORK CITY
MO 6-0160

Not to be noted for its uniqueness of cuisine or decor, the Fairmont Viennese is an average restaurant serving moderately good food at modest prices. A favorite with Columbia students confined to low budgets, the restaurant is generous with its portions of dishes which range from ravioli to sauerbraten. The Stuffed Green Peppers below make a pleasant, satisfying, economical meal; the Apple Strudel is delicious.

STUFFED GREEN PEPPERS (SERVES 6)

12 green peppers
1 medium onion, chopped
2 cloves garlic, minced
2 tablespoons vegetable oil
2 pounds ground beef
⅓ cup rice
   salt
   pepper

Clean peppers and remove seeds, keeping peppers intact.
Sauté onions and garlic in vegetable oil, until onions are golden. Combine onions and garlic with meat and rice. Season with salt and pepper and mix well. Stuff peppers with this mixture and place in saucepan. Cover with water and simmer, covered,

until meat is cooked and peppers are tender (about 45 minutes).
Serve with Tomato Sauce (see below).

TOMATO SAUCE

1 onion, chopped
1 tablespoon oil
2 tablespoons flour
1 cup water
4 tablespoons tomato paste
  salt
  pepper

Sauté onions in oil. Add flour and blend well. Add water, tomato paste, salt and pepper. Mix well and simmer until sauce is
thick and well blended.

APPLE STRUDEL

1 package strudel dough
6 tablespoons melted butter
8 tablespoons sugar
6 tablespoons bread crumbs
3 tablespoons finely chopped nuts or macaroon crumbs
20 ounces canned apple slices or chips
¼ cup red raisins
¼ cup yellow raisins
½ teaspoon cinnamon

Lay out a sheet of strudel dough on damp cloth. Spread with
half the above quantities of butter, sugar and bread crumbs.
Lay second sheet of dough over first and cover with remaining

butter, sugar and bread crumbs. Sprinkle with nuts or macaroon crumbs.

Place apples in a row 2 inches wide and 2 inches from near edge of dough. Sprinkle with raisins and cinnamon. Fold edge of dough over apples and roll carefully to the end, using towel to guide the dough.

Gently transfer strudel to a buttered baking dish and bake at 400° for ½ hour.

FOO JOY

13 DIVISION STREET
NEW YORK CITY
431-4931

Foo Joy is a pleasantly decorated restaurant just across the street from the large Confucius Plaza housing project. The specialty of the house is Fukien cuisine—food from the Chinese coastal province of Fukien. Expect plenty of fish and a respectable amount of spice. We thought the uniqueness of the style might lie in a special use of spices, but owner Pong Fung Pang maintained that texture contrast is the key: "crispy outside and tender inside." The Fukien Pork Chops with Scallion Sauce embody this principle, but the Steamed Fish and Lemon Chicken are distinctive in other ways.

FUKIEN PORK CHOPS WITH SCALLION SAUCE
(SERVES 2)

6 tablespoons cornstarch
¼ cup water
1½ pounds thinly sliced pork chops
    vegetable oil

SCALLION SAUCE

    5 tablespoons soy sauce
    2 tablespoons vinegar
    1 tablespoon A-1 Sauce
    1 tablespoon ketchup
    1 teaspoon sesame oil
       drop Tabasco
    1 tablespoon sugar
       pinch of spicy powder
       pinch of crushed red peppers
    ½ teaspoon salt
    1 scallion, chopped

Combine cornstarch with water, and coat pork chops. Deep-fry pork chops in *very* hot vegetable oil until golden brown. Combine remaining ingredients to form sauce, pour over pork chops and serve.

STEAMED FISH (SERVES 2 TO 4)

    ½ cup salad oil
    ½ tomato, chopped
    2 tablespoons chopped onion
    2 tablespoons green peas
    ½ tablespoon minced ginger
    ½ tablespoon minced garlic
       pinch of crushed red peppers
       Scallion Sauce (see Pork Chop recipe above)
    1 tablespoon cornstarch dissolved in ¼ cup cold water
    1 medium sea bass, steamed

Heat oil. Add tomato, onion, peas, ginger, garlic and peppers. Sauté over a very high flame for a minute. Add Scallion Sauce and heat another minute. Add cornstarch, mix well and serve hot over steamed fish.

LEMON CHICKEN (SERVES 2)

1 pound boned, diced chicken
¼ lemon, minced (including rind)
½ teaspoon minced ginger
1 teaspoon salt
1 teaspoon spicy powder (available in Chinese groceries)
1½ teaspoons sugar
1 ounce sherry
pinch of black pepper
¼ teaspoon sesame oil
1 tablespoon cornstarch

Combine all ingredients and mix well. Steam, covered, over boiling water for 15 minutes.

FOOD

127 PRINCE STREET
NEW YORK CITY
260-3730

Since its opening as an artists' restaurant collective in 1970, Food has passed through many hands. Yet the name and the basic style of the restaurant have remained unchanged. The food is wholesome, imaginative and modestly priced; the staff is cheerful, informal and friendly. Dee Smires and Dan Mayberry are the latest young owners, and they are doing an excellent job maintaining Food's standards.

We obtained the recipes below from Food's extensive recipe collection. Not all the dishes are in the current repertoire, but they are all excellent preparations, and may reappear on the menu.

CORN CHOWDER

6 strips bacon, diced
1 cup diced onions
2 cups diced potatoes
water
2 cups canned sweet corn
1½ cups milk
Tabasco
Worcestershire Sauce
salt
pepper
chopped parsley

Sauté bacon pieces. Add onions and sauté till light brown. Add potatoes and sauté a few minutes longer. Cover with water and simmer till potatoes are tender. Add corn and bring soup to a boil again. Add milk and simmer a few minutes longer. Season and serve.

To make a thicker soup, use part of the milk to prepare a white sauce. Stir in at the end.

HOT AND SOUR SOUP (SERVES 4)

4 mushrooms, sliced thin
4 scallions, chopped
¼ pound lean pork, shredded
2 bean curd cakes, diced
5 cups pork or chicken stock
1 tablespoon sherry
2 tablespoons white vinegar
1 teaspoon salt
1 teaspoon soy sauce
2 tablespoons cornstarch
¼ cup cold water
1 egg, beaten
few drops sesame oil
Optional: 1 cup thinly sliced Chinese vegetables

Bring mushrooms, scallions, pork and bean curd to a boil in stock. Cover and simmer for about 10 minutes, until pork is tender. Add sherry, vinegar, salt and soy sauce.

Dissolve cornstarch in water. Remove about 1 cup of broth from soup and mix well with cornstarch and water. Return this to the soup, stirring in well. Simmer another minute or two.

Remove soup from heat. Add beaten egg and stir in well. Allow soup to sit, covered, for a minute or two. Add sesame oil and serve.

GROUND NUT STEW (SERVES 4)

3 pounds chicken, cut into serving pieces
4 to 5 tablespoons vegetable oil
1 large onion, diced
2 cups chicken stock
2 bay leaves
1 teaspoon salt
¼ teaspoon pepper
6 ounces peanut butter (natural is best; Food uses "Mrs. Smith's")
1 pound okra, steamed
4 or 5 carrots, sliced and steamed
¼ teaspoon Tabasco
3 hard-boiled eggs, chopped
¾ cup chopped scallions
¾ cup chopped parsley
¾ cup fresh peanuts

Brown chicken pieces in oil. Remove.

Sauté onions until golden.

Place chicken and onions in large, heavy pot. Cover with stock. Add bay leaves, salt and pepper. Cover and simmer gently for 1 hour, until chicken is tender. Add peanut butter, okra and carrots. Stir in well and simmer for 15 minutes. Stir occasionally to make sure the peanut butter dissolves. Season with Tabasco. Garnish with eggs, scallions, parsley and peanuts.

BRANDIED DUCK WITH FRUIT STUFFING (SERVES 4)

1 duck
  salt
  cayenne pepper
1 large onion, chopped
3 or 4 pineapple rings (canned is okay)
1 orange, sliced
2 stalks celery, chopped
¼ cup orange juice
½ teaspoon lemon juice
¼ cup brandy
½ teaspoon Tabasco

Remove giblets from duck and reserve for Giblet Rice (see below). Remove excess fat from inside duck and discard.

Rub outside and inside of duck with salt and cayenne pepper. (This helps melt the fat and make the skin crisper.)

Combine remaining ingredients, reserving one pineapple ring and one orange slice. Stuff the duck with the mixture.

Bake, uncovered, at 475° for 20 minutes, or until duck begins to brown.

Remove from oven and pour off fat from bottom of pan, leaving only a little to prevent burning.

Place one pineapple ring and one orange slice on the duck's breast and douse with a little more brandy. Cover with foil and continue to bake at 350° for 1½ hours, pouring off fat every ½ hour.

To serve, remove stuffing, cut duck into quarters and serve with a helping of stuffing, Giblet Rice and steamed broccoli.

GIBLET RICE

1 cup white rice
  giblets of one duck
¼ green pepper, finely chopped
2 or 3 scallions, chopped
2 tablespoons chopped parsley
¼ teaspoon black pepper
  salt to taste

Boil rice with some salt.

Boil giblets until tender. Put through food mill, reserving broth.

Combine giblets with cooked rice and remaining ingredients. Add a few tablespoons of broth to moisten the rice and serve.

SYRIAN COFFEE CAKE

2 cups brown sugar
2 cups sifted white flour
½ cup butter
1 egg
1 teaspoon nutmeg
1 cup sour cream
1 teaspoon baking soda
½ cup chopped nuts

Blend sugar, flour and butter with fingers. Spread half of this crumb mixture in a well-buttered baking dish (9×9 inches).

Stir egg, nutmeg, sour cream and baking soda into remaining crumbs. Mix well and pour over crumbs in baking dish. Cover with chopped nuts. Bake 35 to 40 minutes at 350°.

ICING

1 cup confectioner's sugar
2 tablespoons warm milk
½ teaspoon vanilla

Mix thoroughly and spread over cake.

THE FRONT PORCH

253 WEST 11TH STREET
NEW YORK CITY
243-9262

2272 BROADWAY
NEW YORK CITY
787-9586

*First there was one. Then there were two. Then three. Then four.
Then none.*

Now there are two again.

*Opened in 1971 by Cleves Rich and Liz Zimmerman, The Front
Porch was renowned for its economical and imaginative soups,
breads and desserts personally prepared by the two women. Success brought expansion, and the women set up a commissary
where they began to mass-produce their dishes and ship them to
the various outlets. The commissary was a financial disaster, and
the women were forced to close the business.*

*Not long after the chain closed, some friends purchased part
of the operation and The Front Porch was restored. The staff,
the menu and the decor are unchanged. What's more, the cooking
is now done in the kitchen of each restaurant, under the supervision of Liz and Cleves. Their recipes are outstanding.*

COLD PURPLE PLUM SOUP (SERVES 4)

    1 1-pound or 14-ounce can pitted purple plums
 1½ cups dairy sour cream
   ¼ teaspoon ground cloves
   ½ cup cream sherry
       cinnamon to taste

Liz Zimmerman and Cleves Rich, eating their beautiful and tasty creations at The Front Porch.

Blend all ingredients in a blender for approximately 1 minute until smooth and creamy. Serve chilled.

BEEF OKRA (SERVES 8 TO 10)

```
    2  pounds lean raw chunks of beef, diced
   ¼  pound butter
    4  cups canned tomatoes
 1½  pounds fresh or frozen okra, cut crosswise
       boiling water
    2  cups cooked lima beans
    2  cups diced cooked chicken
    1  tablespoon basil
    2  teaspoons thyme
       salt and pepper to taste
```

In a deep kettle, brown meat in butter. Add tomatoes and okra. Cover with boiling water and simmer, covered, for 1 hour.

Add 4 cups boiling water. Bring to boiling point again, lower heat and simmer covered, stirring frequently. Skim soup. Cook till okra and tomatoes are soft. Add limas and diced chicken. Season with basil, thyme, salt and pepper.

VEAL STEW WITH MUSHROOMS (SERVES 6 TO 8)

```
 2½  pounds boneless veal cubes
    7  medium onions, quartered; stick each quarter with 1 whole
       clove
    2  carrots, sliced into thin circles
    1  tablespoon fresh lemon juice
```

        4 cups water
        1 bay leaf
        1 pound small mushrooms
        4 egg yolks
        1 cup heavy cream
          minced parsley
    1½ teaspoons salt
      ½ teaspoon pepper

Place veal cubes, onions, carrots, lemon juice and bay leaf in a large pot. Cover with water and simmer, covered, until veal is tender (1½ to 2 hours).

Add mushrooms and simmer another 15 to 20 minutes until mushrooms are cooked.

Beat egg yolks and cream. Add about 1 cup of hot broth to this mixture and beat well. Add to soup. Add parsley, salt and pepper, and serve.

LEMON CHESS PIE

        2 cups sugar
        1 tablespoon yellow corn meal
        1 tablespoon flour
        1 pinch salt
      ¼ cup melted butter
      ¼ cup milk
        4 eggs
          juice and grated rind of 2 lemons

Mix sugar, corn meal, flour and salt. Add butter, milk, eggs, lemon juice and rind. Beat well for 1 minute. Pour into unbaked pie shell. Bake at 350° for 40 minutes.

PECAN PRALINE CAKE (SERVES 16 OR MORE)

2 cups buttermilk
1 cup melted butter
4 cups light brown sugar
4 eggs
4 cups flour
2¾ teaspoons baking soda
¼ cup cocoa
2¾ teaspoons vanilla

Warm buttermilk and butter in saucepan.

Add sugar and eggs and beat well. Pour into bowl.

Combine flour, baking soda and cocoa. Add to liquid mixture and beat well. Add vanilla.

Pour into well-greased rectangular pan. Bake at 350° for 25 minutes.

TOPPING

Mix in order:
1 cup melted butter
2 cups light brown sugar
¾ cup (1 small can) evaporated milk
2 cups chopped pecans

When cake is done, spread Topping over cake and return to oven to brown.

BOURECK

3 pounds feta cheese
3 pounds ricotta cheese
4 eggs
⅓ cup chopped parsley
  salt and pepper to taste
2 pounds filo
1 pound butter, melted

Crumble feta cheese and combine with ricotta, beaten eggs and chopped parsley. Season with salt and pepper.

Carefully lay out a sheet of filo. Brush with melted butter. Place a second sheet over the first and brush again with butter. Finally lay a third sheet and brush with butter. Fold in half lengthwise. Brush with butter. Place a heaping tablespoon of the cheese mixture on one end of the rectangle, and fold edge over cheese to form a triangle. Continue folding until you reach the end of the sheet and have formed a well-sealed triangular packet. Repeat this process until you have used all the filo and all the filling.

Brush the top of each packet with butter and arrange in greased baking dish. Bake at 350° until golden (about 20 minutes).

Boureck may be prepared in advance and stored frozen before baking.

GEFEN'S DAIRY RESTAURANT

297 SEVENTH AVENUE
NEW YORK CITY
WA 4-1977

Mr. Farber, owner of Gefen's Dairy Restaurant, stoutly maintained that he had no unique recipes he could give us for this book—"Everyone knows how to make a roast," he insisted. When we pressed him further, however, he relented and admitted that his recipe for pastry dough was a good one. So here it is. If you've ever longed to make traditional Jewish pastries and you don't have a Jewish grandmother to show you how, this recipe is for you.

BASIC PASTRY DOUGH (FOR DANISHES, BUTTER HORNS, ETC.) (MAKES ABOUT 25 PASTRIES)

    2 eggs
 ½ cup sugar
1½ teaspoons salt
 ¼ cup milk
 ¼ cup water
2½ cups sifted flour
 ½ teaspoon baking powder
 ½ cup oil

Beat eggs, sugar and salt. Add milk and water, and mix well. Add 1 cup flour and baking powder; blend. Add ½ cup flour and mix well. Blend in oil; then add final cup of flour and mix thoroughly. Be sure to handle this dough gently, mixing only until all ingredients are blended. Carefully roll out to ¼-inch thickness and cut into rectangles, approximately 2×3 inches.

To make butter horns, brush dough with melted butter. Sprinkle with cinnamon, sugar and raisins. Roll into crescents, coat with egg and bake at 350° until golden. When finished and still hot, brush with sugar water.

For cheese Danishes, place a mixture of pot cheese, butter, cream cheese and sugar on each rectangle. Fold all four corners over the filling, coat with egg and bake as above. The proportions for the filling are up to you.

Prune Danishes may be made simply by placing prunes on the dough, folding over 2 diagonal corners and baking as above.

GOURMET ON THE RUN

129 EAST 28TH STREET
NEW YORK CITY
685-0256

Gourmet on the Run, or "My Mother's Place," is the kind of restaurant many women—those who've always been told by well-fed friends and relatives, "You're such a good cook, you should open a restaurant"—dream of owning. It's rare that such an establishment gets off the ground, and even rarer when the restaurant preserves the quality and feel of the home cooking that inspired it. Mrs. Visconti, however, has managed to do just that. Her restaurant is small, her kitchen tiny, her staff almost nonexistent . . . and the food is delicious, the dining comfortable, the atmosphere distinctly "at home."

All the offerings at "My Mother's Place" are unique preparations developed by Mrs. Visconti. Her cooking style is very simple, since she wisely refuses to waste time or energy . . . yet the results are delicious and satisfying. Stuffed Chicken Breasts—a modest misnomer for a simple but elegant chicken extravaganza—seems to be completely without precedent. The Torta de Crema is an outstanding dessert—delicious and very easy to prepare.

EGGPLANT SICILIAN (SERVES 4 TO 6)

Marinara Sauce (see below)
1 eggplant, sliced very thin (⅛ to ¼ inch)
garlic powder
garlic salt

Gourmet on the Run

Parmesan cheese (grated)
seasoned bread crumbs
coarsely grated mozzarella cheese

Ladle some Marinara Sauce into the bottom of a shallow baking dish. Cover with a layer of eggplant. Sprinkle with garlic powder, garlic salt, Parmesan and seasoned bread crumbs. Cover with another spoonful of sauce. Flatten out, and add another layer of eggplant. Repeat until all eggplant is used.

Bake 25 minutes in 400° oven. Sprinkle with mozzarella and return to oven for another 10 minutes.

MARINARA SAUCE

¾ cup olive oil
 2 cloves garlic, minced
    handful of oregano
 1 2-pound can Italian peeled tomatoes with basil
 1 teaspoon salt
    black pepper to taste
    dash of sherry or white wine

Heat olive oil and garlic just until garlic becomes aromatic; do not brown. Add oregano and heat a few minutes longer. Now add tomatoes, squeezing each tomato gently in your hand before adding. Add salt, pepper and wine. Cover and simmer 20 to 30 minutes. (Cover should not be tight, but should allow some steam to escape.) Skim any oil that comes to the top.

STUFFED CHICKEN BREASTS (4 SERVINGS)

2 whole, boneless chicken breasts
2 eggs
2 cups milk
  seasoned bread crumbs
  butter
  garlic powder
  onion powder
1½ cups shredded or coarsely grated mozzarella cheese
4 or 8 very thin slices Genoa salami or ham
  black pepper
½ to ¾ cup grated Parmesan cheese

Wash chicken well and pat dry. Split each breast in half and remove any gristle or bones.

Beat eggs with ½ cup milk. Dip each breast into eggs and milk, then into bread crumbs, making sure they are well coated.

Lay chicken breasts in well-buttered baking dish (or use individual dish for each serving). Place a pat of butter under each breast.

Sprinkle each breast generously with garlic powder and onion powder. Cover with mozzarella. Now cover with slices of salami or ham and sprinkle with freshly ground black pepper.

Combine remaining milk with balance of beaten milk and eggs. Add bread crumbs and Parmesan to create a liquid but fairly rich batter. Mix well and pour over each breast. Top each with a lump of butter.

Bake in a very hot oven (400 to 450°) until top is golden brown (about 20 to 25 minutes, depending on how good your oven is). Serve immediately. Also excellent cold.

TORTA DE CREMA (10 INDIVIDUAL TARTS)

  1 pint ricotta cheese
 ½ pint fudge twirl or vanilla ice cream
  1 tablespoon sugar
 ½ teaspoon cinnamon or to taste
  3 drops vanilla extract
 ¼ cup chopped milk chocolate
    handful slivered almonds
    cognac, Grand Marnier, coffee, sherry, Kahlua or any other
       flavoring to taste

 10 small graham cracker shells, or one large graham cracker
       piecrust

Combine first 8 ingredients and beat gently by hand. Spoon into piecrust and freeze. Remove from freezer at least ten minutes before serving. Top with whipped cream.

This is an amazingly simple, delicious dessert. After you've made it the first time, you should find infinite ways of changing the basic recipe, adding candied fruit, different nuts, liqueurs, etc. Preparation time is less than ten minutes, and the tarts can always be kept frozen and ready to serve whenever the mood hits you (which is likely to be very often). The dessert is not as caloric as many others we know of, and may also be made successfully with dietetic ingredients.

THE GRAND DAIRY RESTAURANT

341 GRAND STREET
NEW YORK CITY
261-0503

The Grand Dairy Restaurant, located on a busy corner on Grand Street, looks as if it's been in the same spot serving the same home-style Jewish food for 20 or 30 years. In fact, it's been around for less than 10 years, although its air of antiquity may be a clue to its success. Owned and managed by the amiable Sol Guberman, the Grand would not be what it is without its highly verbal staff of Jewish-restaurant old-timers. Charlie and Irving ("the Sage") are always on hand at the counter to make some jokes and urge you to eat more. Chef Eddie Weiser has been in the "food business" for 45 years and boasts a Gefulte Fish good enough to please any Grandma-makes-it-best diehard. While Eddie insists that the secret of a good restaurant is the ability to make good coffee and soup, Irving insists that it's TLC (Tender Loving Care). Whatever it is, the Grand has it.

MUSHROOM BARLEY SOUP (SERVES 8 TO 10)

1 pound pearl barley
2 tablespoons coarse salt
⅜ cup sugar
2 carrots, ground or grated
1 stalk celery, ground or grated
1 onion, ground or grated
½ pound fresh mushrooms, sliced

5 quarts water
2 potatoes, diced
¼ pound sweet butter
   freshly chopped dill

Combine all ingredients except potatoes, butter and dill. Bring to a boil, cover and cook over medium heat for ¾ hour. Lower heat and simmer 15 minutes. Add potatoes. Simmer another 30 to 45 minutes, stirring occasionally to keep barley from sticking. Add butter at end and blend in thoroughly. Sprinkle with dill and serve.

GEFULTE FISH (SERVES 18)

4 pounds whitefish
1 pound pike   } (or 5 pounds whitefish)
4 onions
1 cup matzoh meal
8 eggs
¼ cup seltzer
½ cup water
2 tablespoons pepper
3 tablespoons sugar
2 tablespoons coarse salt

6 quarts water
6 onions, sliced
2 carrots, sliced
¾ cup sugar
⅜ cup coarse salt
2 tablespoons pepper

Remove bones from fish and grind fish and onions very fine.

Combine fish, matzoh meal, eggs, seltzer, water, 2 tablespoons pepper, 3 tablespoons sugar and 2 tablespoons salt. Mix well and beat for about 15 minutes. Taste and adjust seasoning. Shape into balls or oblongs.

Bring water, sliced onions, carrots, ¾ cup sugar, ⅜ cup salt and 2 tablespoons pepper to a boil and simmer until carrots are soft. Drop fish into water, bring to a boil again, then simmer, covered, for 2 hours. Remove fish from liquid. Strain liquid. Place fish in pot or large dish and cover with clear liquid. Refrigerate. Can keep for 2 weeks. (As a garnish, you may add boiled sliced carrots to the liquid, which will jell around the fish.)

BAKED GEFULTE FISH

1 16-ounce can tomato purée
1 16-ounce can tomatoes (squeeze tomatoes to break them up)
1 orange juice can vegetable oil
1 tablespoon coarse salt
3 tablespoons sugar
2 tablespoons cornstarch dissolved in ½ cup cold water

Combine first 5 ingredients and bring to a boil. Add dissolved cornstarch and simmer for 5 minutes.

Cover Gefulte Fish with sauce and place in 350° oven for 5 minutes. Reduce heat to 270° and bake another 5 minutes. Now reduce heat to 200° and bake 10 minutes longer. Serve.

This sauce may also be used as a topping for any other baked fish.

NOODLE PUDDING (SERVES 20)

2 pounds medium egg noodles
8 to 10 eggs
2½ cups sugar
¼ cup raisins
1 tablespoon coarse salt
¼ pound melted butter
1 tablespoon vanilla or orange flavoring

Boil noodles and drain.

Combine remaining ingredients and beat well. Add noodles and mix well. Place in lightly greased baking dish. Bake 15 minutes at 400°. Reduce heat to 200° and bake another hour. Let cool at least 5 minutes before serving.

FRUIT SALAD (SERVES 12)

5 Sunkist oranges, peeled
1 white grapefruit, peeled
2 pink grapefruits, peeled
1 apple
¼ pound seedless grapes
3 quarts water
¾ pound sugar
1 teaspoon sour salt

Dice fruit and combine with water, sugar and sour salt. Can keep in refrigerator up to 1 week.

GREEN TREE

1034 AMSTERDAM AVENUE
NEW YORK CITY
864–9106

Green Tree is a professionally run Hungarian restaurant catering primarily to Columbia students and other penny-savers on the Upper West Side. Its offerings are generous, cheap (especially at lunch) and out-of-the-ordinary. The Goulash recipe below is a particularly delicious version of the classic beef stew. There's more paprika in Mr. Kende's recipe than in most, but that just makes it taste better. In fact, you should bring some paprika to the table along with the salt, to make the dish even more Hungarian. Palacsinta recipes vary from chef to chef; this is a light and tasty one.

HUNGARIAN GOULASH (SERVES 6 TO 8)

½ cup vegetable oil
4 pounds beef shank, cut into large cubes for stewing
1 pound onions, chopped
1½ green peppers, chopped
½ teaspoon garlic powder
¾ teaspoon white pepper
2½ teaspoons MSG
1¼ teaspoons salt
4 teaspoons paprika
1½ tablespoons ketchup
1 cup water

Heat the oil and brown the meat on all sides. Add the vegetables, seasonings and water. Cover and simmer over very low heat for 2½ hours.

If you like, the sauce may be thickened with a teaspoon or two of cornstarch, dissolved first in some cold water.

BRAINS WITH EGGS (SERVES 2)

4 tablespoons brains, chopped
2 tablespoons chopped onions
2 teaspoons butter
4 eggs
  salt
  paprika

Sauté brains and onions in butter for two minutes. Add eggs and cook as scrambled eggs. Season with salt and paprika.

PALACSINTA (MAKES ABOUT 16 PANCAKES, TO SERVE 8)

2 cups milk
3 cups flour
2 eggs
1 cup sugar
½ teaspoon salt
1½ to 2 cups water as needed to make a light batter
  vegetable oil

Combine all ingredients (except oil). Heat frying pan and grease lightly with vegetable oil. Pour a thin layer of batter onto pan, and fry over a very high flame for about ½ minute. Turn and brown on second side.

Use apricot jam, chopped walnuts or cottage cheese mixed with egg yolk, sugar and vanilla as the filling. To serve, place pancake on a plate and put some filling along center. Roll pancake around filling and sprinkle with confectioner's sugar.

HAMMER'S DAIRY RESTAURANT

243 EAST 14TH STREET
NEW YORK CITY
473–9805

Hammer's Dairy Restaurant is a living landmark, a thriving remnant of an earlier era and a different culture. Many businesses have come and gone on East 14th Street, but Hammer's has maintained its place since 1913, when it was opened by the young Mr. and Mrs. Hammer.

The pace at Hammer's these days is slow and comfortable; bread baskets are routinely filled and refilled with fresh rolls and breads of various textures and colors; water is quietly and regularly replenished. No one in the restaurant is rushing to go anywhere; there is no striving to please or succeed. Yet success for the restaurant and pleasure for the customers result. Mrs. Hammer is still taking care of the cooking, which is excellent. The restaurant's survival is a tribute to her strength and will; she is completely unselfconscious, however, about her success and modest about her skill. "There's nothing to it," she says about the cooking, which is simple, economical and tasty.

PICKLED FISH (SERVES 4 TO 6)

2 pounds haddock, pike, or salmon, in 1-inch slices
1 large onion, sliced
1 or 2 carrots, sliced
1 stalk celery, sliced
2 quarts water

1 cup vinegar
2 to 3 tablespoons sugar
  juice of 1 lemon
2 tablespoons mixed (pickling) spice

Place fish, onion, carrots, celery and water in large pot. Bring to boil and simmer, covered, for 15 to 20 minutes. Add vinegar, sugar and lemon juice. Continue to simmer for 1 to 1½ hours. Add mixed spice and simmer another 5 minutes.

Let fish and broth cool. Remove fish from broth and place in rectangular pan. Strain broth and pour over fish, adding a few carrot and onion slices to the pan. Refrigerate until broth jells. Serve cold.

MAMALIGA (SERVES 2)

3 cups water
  pinch salt
  pinch sugar
1 cup yellow corn meal
4 tablespoons butter
½ cup cottage cheese

Bring water to a boil with salt and sugar. Slowly stir in corn meal. Bring to a second boil and simmer for 10 minutes. Stir occasionally.

To serve, place corn meal in bowls. Cover with butter and cottage cheese.

VEGETABLE SOUP (SERVES 12)

3 carrots, diced
1 cup string beans, cut into 1-inch pieces
1 cup green peas
1 onion, diced
1 stalk celery, diced
2 parsnips, diced
1 cup cauliflower, broken into pieces
2 gallons water
2 potatoes, diced
1 onion, diced
2 tablespoons butter
   salt
   pepper

Simmer first 7 vegetables in water for 1½ to 2 hours. Add potatoes and continue to simmer another 15 minutes. Sauté onion in butter and add to soup. Season with salt and pepper and serve.

FRUIT SOUP (SERVES 8)

½ pound dried mixed fruit (prunes, plums, apricots, pears, peaches)
2 quarts water

2 pounds mixed fresh fruit (grapes, cherries, pineapple,
    peaches, plums)
  juice of ½ lemon
½ cup sugar

Simmer dried fruit in water for 15 minutes. Add fresh fruit
and simmer another 15 minutes. Add lemon juice and sugar.
Stir in well. Let cool, refrigerate and serve cold.

HEE SEUNG FUNG TEAHOUSE-RESTAURANT

46–48 BOWERY
NEW YORK CITY
374-1319

Hee Seung Fung is a bustling teahouse/restaurant, serving both Cantonese main dishes and the unique "dim sum" delicacies. Dim sum are served from 9 A.M. to 5 P.M. and are properly consumed as lunch or afternoon snacks, accompanied by large quantities of tea. (At Hee Seung Fung there is a choice of five different teas.) The dim sum are complex, varied creations, difficult to define within Western categories. Some are dumplings; some are cakes or custards; others are more like pastries. Each is an entity unto itself, and they all require patience and care to prepare.

Ming Chen, the young owner of Hee Seung Fung, was very precise in explaining the following recipes to us. He is fully versed in the proper techniques, having worked in a Chinese kitchen for 12 years prior to coming to New York. (He began this work when he was 8 years old.) He continues to do much of the cooking at his restaurant, and is an enthusiastic proponent of the dim sum tradition. The following recipes should prove both manageable and exciting.

HAR GOW (SHRIMP DUMPLINGS) (MAKES 8 DOZEN TINY DUMPLINGS)

1 cup water
1 pound wheat starch
1 tablespoon lard
1 pound shrimp
4 teaspoons salt
2 tablespoons sugar
3 ounces bamboo shoots, very finely chopped

Bring water to a boil. Place wheat starch in a large bowl. Pour boiling water onto starch and mix well with a wooden spoon. When the starch and the water have been well blended, turn dough onto a board and knead well with both hands. Add lard and knead it in. Dough should be soft and rubbery.

Break dough into four sections. Roll each piece out into a cylinder, about 1 foot long and ¾-inch in diameter. Cut each cylinder into ½-inch segments. Cover with a damp towel to prevent drying.

Remove shells from shrimp. Devein and rinse well. Dry thoroughly. Place in large pot or bowl. Add salt and sugar. Now take a handful of shrimp and forcefully throw it back into the pot. Take up another handful and throw it in again. Continue this process until the shrimp is completely crushed and blended with the salt and sugar. This procedure must be performed with energy; *throw* the shrimp into the pot as hard as you can. When the shrimp is completely crushed, add the bamboo shoots and mix in well.

Place a ½-inch cylindrical segment of dough on a clean wooden board. Dip a paper towel in oil and keep it nearby. Flatten the dough with your palm. Touch a rectangular-bladed Chinese knife to the greased towel. Press it against the dough and swing it in short arcs to create a paper-thin circle of dough. Slip the knife under the dough to remove it from the board. (Make sure to keep knife lightly oiled.) Repeat this process with each segment of the dough.

Place about ½ teaspoon of shrimp mixture on each circle of dough. Fold dough over and pinch together to form a crescent-shaped dumpling (imitating the shape of a whole shrimp). Steam the dumplings, covered, over boiling water for 5 minutes. Serve.

LO BA KO (WHITE TURNIP CAKES) (MAKES 18 CAKES)

A large Chinese steamer is necessary.

¼ pound Chinese sausage
¼ pound Chinese dried pork (belly)
¼ pound dried shrimp
1 pound Chinese white turnips
½ pound rice flour
3 cups cold water
¾ teaspoon salt
1⅛ teaspoons sugar
  pinch MSG
2 teaspoons peanut oil

Chop sausage, pork and shrimp into pieces about the size of beans. Grind turnips in meat grinder.

Place rice flour in large bowl. Add water and mix in well, using your hands. Add sausage, pork and shrimp. Add turnips, salt, sugar, MSG and oil. Mix in well.

Heat wok and add turnip mixture. Cook over high flame for 15 minutes, stirring constantly. Pour custard into rectangular baking pan (about 9×12 inches). Flatten surface. Steam, covered, for 1 hour.

Cut turnip cake into small rectangles, about ½-inch deep × 3 inches long × 2 inches wide. Pan-fry on both sides before serving.

CHA SIO BOW (ROAST PORK BUNS) (MAKES ABOUT 40 BUNS)

1 pound roast pork, sliced thin
8 ounces oyster sauce
1 pound white flour
¼ pound sugar
4 teaspoons yeast
1 cup water

Cut pork into ½-inch squares. Combine with oyster sauce and mix well.

Combine flour and sugar. Add yeast. Add water and mix well to form a light dough. Break dough into ½-ounce sections. Shape into balls; then roll out to form flat circles.

Place 1 teaspoon of pork mixture on each piece of dough. Fold dough around pork to form a sphere. Steam for 15 minutes, leaving plenty of space between buns, since the dough puffs to form large balls.

FUNG WONG KO (PHOENIX MEAT PIES) (MAKES 16 PIES)

½ pound shrimp
½ pound pork
¼ teaspoon salt
⅜ teaspoon sugar
¼ teaspoon MSG
6 eggs
  peanut oil

Remove shells from shrimp. Devein, wash and dry well. Dice pork and shrimp into ¼-inch cubes. Place in large bowl with salt, sugar and MSG. Take up a handful of mixture, then throw it vigorously into the bowl. Continue this process until the mixture becomes sticky and holds together.

Divide pork/shrimp mixture into 1-ounce sections. Shape into narrow rectangles, about 3 inches × ½ inch × ½ inch. Steam for 5 minutes.

Beat eggs. Dip steamed pork/shrimp pies into eggs. Pan-fry in a small amount of oil and serve.

Owners Teli and George Kletsidis display a sea bass on their well-worn chopping block in the Hellenic Palace kitchen.

HELLENIC PALACE

250 WEST 27TH STREET
NEW YORK CITY
246-5266

Duplicating the Hellenic Palace's dishes at home requires much more time and effort than most modern households lavish on food preparation, but the results and the experience itself make the process worthwhile. Greek cooking requires numerous stages and subpreparations which are only gradually combined into the final creation. It is an extremely sophisticated style, with careful attention given to details of taste, color and texture.

Spinach Pie in particular is a lesson in patience: you must boil the spinach, prepare a white sauce, sauté the onions and scallions, combine the spinach with the cheese, then finally roll your triangular packets . . . then bake them. Hardly an enterprise for the frozen-food addict. But for those who consider the kitchen as a workshop, where the relaxed craftsman can putter away for hours with complete contentment, the project is a must. Time moves slowly, your hands work peacefully, your eye is gratified by the changing colors and textures. It's a good way to spend an afternoon, and the result is definitely a creation to be proud of. If you don't already enjoy the pleasures of the kitchen, let this be your introduction.

SPANAKOTIROPITA (SPINACH PIE) (MAKES ABOUT 20 INDIVIDUAL PIES)

1 pound spinach
2 onions, chopped
1 bunch scallions, chopped
1 tablespoon olive oil
½ pound butter, melted
   salt
   pepper
1 pound feta cheese, broken into small pieces
8 eggs
1 cup white sauce, with some Parmesan cheese and nutmeg
   added
1 pound filo

Wash spinach and boil until tender. Strain and chop fine.

Sauté onions and scallions in 1 tablespoon oil and 1 tablespoon butter. When onions are golden, add spinach, salt and pepper to taste, and cook gently for another 5 minutes.

In a large bowl, combine spinach mixture with feta, beaten eggs and white sauce. Let cool.

To roll: Gently open out a sheet of filo. Brush lightly with melted butter and fold into thirds lengthwise. Spread butter along the length. Fold up bottom edge of dough to meet side, forming a triangle. Open. Place a generous spoonful or two of spinach mixture in space above diagonal. Fold bottom up again, over spinach, and holding triangle closed, continue to fold triangle up along length of dough. (Check a Boy Scout manual for the correct way of folding the American flag—the technique is the same.) Repeat this procedure with each sheet of filo, until you have used all the dough and all the filling.

Place closed packets on well-buttered baking dish. Brush tops with butter and bake 20 minutes at 350°, until filo is crisp and golden. Serve hot, as an appetizer or side dish.

PASTITSIO (SERVES 6 TO 8)

```
 1  pound ziti
 ½  pound ground beef
 ½  pound ground lamb
 2  onions, chopped
 2  tablespoons butter
 2  cups stewed tomatoes
 ½  cup tomato paste
 3  bay leaves
 ½  stick cinnamon
 ½  cup white wine
    salt
    pepper
 2  eggs, beaten
 ¼  cup grated Parmesan cheese
 ¼  cup bread crumbs
 1  cup white sauce
```

Boil ziti until half cooked. Strain and rinse in cold water.

Sauté meat and onions in butter, 10 to 15 minutes. Add tomatoes, tomato paste, bay leaves, cinnamon and wine. Season with salt and pepper. Simmer, covered, for 1 hour. Skim fat and remove bay leaves and cinnamon stick.

Combine ziti with meat sauce. Add beaten eggs and cheese, and mix well.

Butter 9×13-inch baking dish and sprinkle with bread crumbs. Spread meat-and-pasta mixture in pan, then cover with white sauce. Cover pan with aluminum foil and bake 30 minutes in 400° oven, or until top is golden brown.

SKODALIA (SERVES 4 TO 6)

    1 pound potatoes
    ½ head garlic, peeled
    ½ teaspoon salt
    2 tablespoons vinegar
    1 tablespoon olive oil
 2½ tablespoons mayonnaise

Boil peeled potatoes in salted water until tender. Drain, mash and beat well in electric mixer.

Using a mortar and pestle, mash garlic cloves with salt. Slowly add 2 teaspoons vinegar, beating until you have a thick paste. Add remainder of vinegar and beat well. Press this mixture through a strainer. Add olive oil and beat well.

Beat vinegar/garlic/oil mixture into potatoes, using electric mixer. Now beat in mayonnaise until potatoes are creamy and smooth. Taste and adjust seasoning with salt, garlic or vinegar. Press potatoes through pastry bag to form a decorative appetizer. Serve cold, garnished with olives, pickled beets and pimentos.

HERSHEY'S DAIRY RESTAURANT

167 WEST 29TH STREET
NEW YORK CITY
LA 4-5389

Hershey's Dairy Restaurant may look like a completely modern restaurant/delicatessen, but it is in fact a relic of the past, when the neighboring streets were bustling with furriers and the dairy restaurant was a more common Jewish institution. Today there are few exclusively dairy restaurants left in the city, but Hershey's continues to maintain the dairy traditions of high-quality, high-calorie dairy food. In business for over 20 years, the restaurant has a faithful following of old regulars.

Hershey's chef, Asnat Bakshi, has been with the restaurant for over 8 years. Like many New York restaurant chefs, she developed her cooking skills without any formal training. Twenty-five years ago she was living in Israel and desperate for work. She got a dishwashing position, and for six months she secretly studied the techniques of the Hungarian cook she worked with. Confident that she could duplicate her mentor's efforts, she joined the Israeli cooks' union and immediately began preparing meals for the staff of a large Israeli hotel. She's been cooking ever since and has become an expert in Israeli, Arab, Russian and Jewish dairy food. Every morning at Hershey's, she personally prepares all the day's offerings, working quickly and neatly, emerging from the kitchen by 11 A.M. in a spotless white uniform. She never tastes her preparations, nor does she measure ingredients: "You can tell whether something is good just by looking and smelling," she says.

BORSCHT (SERVES 4)

6 large beets, grated
1 quart water
1 teaspoon salt
1 tablespoon sugar
1½ teaspoons sour salt
2 eggs, beaten
3 tablespoons sour cream

Boil beets in water with salt, sugar and sour salt for at least 1 hour.

Remove borscht from heat and slowly stir in eggs and sour cream. Blend well. Adjust seasoning to taste. Refrigerate and serve very cold.

VEGETABLE ROAST (SERVES 4 TO 6)

2 stalks celery, chopped
6 carrots, chopped
6 onions, chopped
3 green peppers, chopped
2 quarts water
handful parsley
handful dill
1 teaspoon salt
¼ teaspoon pepper

2 carrots, grated
2 tablespoons vegetable oil
2 eggs, beaten
½ cup matzoh meal
1 teaspoon salt
½ teaspoon pepper

Boil first 4 vegetables in 2 quarts water with parsley, dill, 1 teaspoon salt and ¼ teaspoon pepper for 1½ hours. Drain and grind.

Sauté grated carrots in vegetable oil. Combine with ground boiled vegetables. Reserve a small amount of beaten eggs for a glaze. Then slowly add remainder of eggs and matzoh meal to vegetables to create a soft paste. Season to taste with salt and pepper. Shape into cakes or a loaf, glaze with beaten egg and bake at 250° for ½ hour.

POTATO PUDDING (SERVES 20)

5 pounds potatoes, grated
1 large onion, grated
2 cups vegetable oil
1 cup flour
  salt
  pepper

Combine all ingredients and bake in 250° oven for 1 hour.

NOODLE PUDDING (SERVES 8)

```
 1  pound noodles
2⅔  cups milk
 ⅔  cup sugar
 3  eggs, well beaten
 ⅔  cup sour cream
 ½  cup raisins
    vanilla extract
 5  ounces butter, melted
```

Boil noodles and rinse in cold water. Combine with other ingredients and stir well. Bake in greased pan for 2 hours at 250°. For rice pudding, use same ingredients in same proportions, substituting boiled rice for the noodles.

HONG YING RICE SHOP

11 MOTT STREET
NEW YORK CITY
349-6126

Originally a small family restaurant, Hong Ying has grown in size and popularity over the years. It seats 140 now, and there are often long lines of customers waiting for the opportunity to sample the restaurant's offerings. Most popular are the low-priced noodle dishes, which come in numerous variations. The restaurant also offers some interesting specialties, including several dishes prepared with golden mushrooms. These are delicate, long-stemmed mushrooms with a light and pleasing flavor. Imported by Hong Ying's owner, they are not available elsewhere.

The Stuffed Boneless Fish below is an unusual Chinese delicacy, beautifully prepared by chef Sing Lee. The process of removing the fish meat from the skin is rather tricky, but can be mastered with patience.

STUFFED BONELESS FISH (SERVES 1 OR 2)

    1 whole sea bass (about 1 pound)
    3 scallions, chopped very fine
 ½ cup black mushrooms, chopped very fine
    4 fresh water chestnuts, chopped very fine
    3 to 4 tablespoons vegetable oil
    1 tablespoon oyster sauce
    2 tablespoons dark soy sauce
    2 tablespoons light soy sauce

4 tablespoons chicken broth
⅛ teaspoon salt
¼ teaspoon sugar
  pinch MSG
1 tablespoon cornstarch dissolved in ¼ cup cold water
1 tablespoon oil
2 teaspoons minced ginger
2 tablespoons scallions, cut in thin strips about 1 inch long

Scrape fish well.

Slit skin along either side of backbone, up to 1 inch from head and tail. Gently peel whole skin away from fish. Carefully remove bones and entrails. Chop meat and combine with chopped scallions, mushrooms and water chestnuts. Carefully stuff mixture back into fish skin.

Heat vegetable oil in wok or skillet. Sear stuffed fish on both sides, cover and cook over low flame 15 to 20 minutes. Remove fish from oil. Clean wok.

Combine oyster sauce, soy, chicken broth, salt, sugar, MSG and dissolved cornstarch. Blend well. Heat 1 tablespoon oil in wok. Sauté ginger and scallion strips for 1 minute. Add sauce and heat thoroughly. Serve over fish.

IDEAL LUNCH AND BAR

238 EAST 86TH STREET
NEW YORK CITY
RH 4-9685

Without striving for effect, the Ideal Lunch and Bar is one of the more inviting restaurant/luncheonettes in New York. The food is solidly German; the staff is unpretentious and casually efficient; the customers are obviously content with their meals and absorbed either in private musings or in friendly conversation. There is a certain matter-of-factness about the establishment which permeates the atmosphere and encourages you to relax and dig into the tasty, plentiful and modestly priced food. Open 7 days from 7 A.M. to midnight, the Ideal draws an interesting mix of customers, from local laborers to business people to old Eastern European immigrants. It is a place where the first-time customer can feel at home, and where regulars can be seen securely occupying their personal "spots" at the time-worn counter or in the small rear dining room. German is the predominant language, although English is accepted.

Ideal's friendly German owner was very much concerned to provide recipes that could be accurately duplicated at home. He explained that the Roulade of Beef, however, might not turn out as tasty as the restaurant's version. At Ideal it is prepared using the restaurant's flavorful and indispensable beef stock . . . a concoction not easily analyzed or reproduced. Home cooks are urged to use whatever beef flavoring they have on hand, and to please forgive the difference.

ROULADE OF BEEF (SERVES 4)

4 slices top round (3×8×⅜ inches)—about 1 pound
4 tablespoons mustard
½ pound ground beef
1 carrot, julienned
1 small onion, sliced lengthwise
1 pickle, julienned
4 bacon strips, fried and drained
  salt
  pepper
¾ to 1 pound beef bones
2 carrots, sliced
1 onion, quartered
2 stalks celery, sliced
2 to 3 cups water or beef stock
  Maggi flavoring, or any beef base or bouillon
2 tablespoons butter
4 tablespoons flour

Place slices of beef on counter. Spread generously with mustard. Place a quarter of the ground beef on each slice, across the width. Cover with carrot, onion, pickle and bacon slices. Roll each piece of beef around the filling and secure with toothpicks or string. Season with salt and pepper.

Grease bottom of roasting pan with beef fat or oil. Arrange beef bones, sliced carrots, quartered onion and celery on bottom of pan. Add beef rolls. Place in 350° oven and roast until beef is browned (about 30 to 45 minutes). Turn rolls to brown evenly.

Add boiling water or stock to pan, just to cover beef. Season to taste with beef base, salt and pepper. Cover. Return to oven and simmer 1½ to 2 hours, until beef is very tender.

Remove beef rolls from baking pan and set aside. Strain stock and skim off fat. In a heavy ovenproof pot, melt butter. Stir in flour and brown over medium heat. Slowly stir in stock and blend well. Adjust seasoning. Add beef rolls and vegetables to gravy. Cover pot and place in 350° oven for 15 minutes. Serve with potatoes or noodles.

GERMAN PANCAKES (SERVES 4)

1½ cups flour
½ to ⅔ cup milk
1 teaspoon sugar
  pinch salt
8 eggs
¼ pound butter

Place flour in large bowl. Slowly stir in milk until mixture becomes a thick paste. Add sugar and salt. Mix well.

Beat eggs until they are frothy. Add to flour-and-milk mixture and beat well.

Melt 2 tablespoons butter in 9- or 10-inch skillet. Pour in a quarter of the batter and fry over medium heat. When bottom is browned and top has begun to set, turn pancake over and fry a few minutes longer. Serve with applesauce.

IDEAL RESTAURANT

2825 BROADWAY
NEW YORK CITY
866-3224

Cuban cooking, as distinct from the Asian-Cuban amalgam, is relatively rare in New York. The Ideal is a good and reasonably priced place to sample this branch of Latin cuisine. Originally a counter operation in modestly utilitarian quarters, the Ideal has expanded into a full-sized restaurant. The walls are brick interspersed with dark wood; green plants and empty Chianti bottles add a festive touch. Owner Frank Castro is usually on hand for some lighthearted conversation with his customers, many of whom still gather at the refurbished counter to exchange neighborhood gossip in English and Spanish. The cook is Elio Gomez, a competent chef also known for his poetry, which is published occasionally in El Tiempo. *Nicknamed "Poeta," Gomez is an aggressive and enterprising cook who enjoys experimenting within the limits of the Latin style. He has many unique preparations for Ideal, including the Filet Mignon on page 158.*

BATIDO (TROPICAL SHAKE)

5 ice cubes, crushed
4 heaping tablespoons papaya or mango pulp
2 heaping tablespoons sugar
milk

Place ice in blender. Add fruit pulp and sugar. Cover with milk and blend, adding more milk if necessary to achieve desired consistency. This delicious drink may be made with any tropical fruit (banana, guanabana, pineapple, mamey, anon, even watermelon), although the proportions vary and you will have to learn what you like by experimenting.

PAELLA (SERVES 2 TO 4)

4 lobster tails
15 shrimp
4 clams
2 crab claws
4 scallops
1 chorizo, sliced
¼ pound chicken, cut into pieces
¼ pound ham, diced
2 tablespoons Spanish olive oil
¼ onion, chopped
½ green pepper, chopped
2 canned tomatoes, peeled and chopped
1 stalk celery, chopped
4 leaves cilantro fino, chopped
1 teaspoon saffron
10 stuffed olives
  oregano
  cumin
  pepper
1 bay leaf
4 cups stock (prepared from beef, chicken, fish bones cooked with onions, peppers, pimentos, etc.)
2 cups rice
1 cup sherry

Sauté all ingredients except stock, rice and sherry in large, heavy casserole for about 10 minutes, seasoning with salt to taste. Add stock and simmer for 10 minutes. Then add rice, bring to a boil and simmer, covered, for 15 minutes. Place casserole in oven and bake at 350° for 30 minutes. Stir occasionally. Just before serving, stir in 1 cup sherry. "Dress" with olives, pimentos, asparagus, mushrooms. Serve and enjoy.

FILET MIGNON IDEAL (SERVES 2)

    4 tablespoons olive oil
 1½ pounds filet mignon, in 1-inch cubes
    ¼ pound ham, diced
    ½ chorizo, sliced
    4 canned, peeled tomatoes, chopped
    ½ green pepper, in strips
    ½ medium onion, sliced
    1 stalk celery, chopped
    ½ small can mushrooms, drained
  10 stuffed olives
    1 ounce Spanish sherry
    ½ tablespoon Spanish paprika
    3 tablespoons chopped parsley
    3 leaves cilantro fino, chopped
    ½ teaspoon salt
    ½ teaspoon MSG

Heat olive oil in large skillet or pot. Throw in all other ingredients and sauté over medium heat, 15 to 20 minutes. Serve with rice and fried bananas.

IDRA

166 WEST 4TH STREET
NEW YORK CITY
691-5667

*Idra is an interesting Greek restaurant, with an unusually large
and reasonably priced menu. The upstairs room bears some resemblance to a garden bower, with a trellis and hanging artificial
flora; in the evenings there is Greek music, played the night we
were there by two expressionless but proficient musicians.*

*The recipes Idra's manager shared with us are exceptional.
The Leg of Lamb is flavorful and tender. Kakavia is a marvelous
fish stew. Galactoboureko is another Mideastern filo creation, and
it is superb. Once you begin preparing desserts with filo you
won't want to make anything else. The dough can be purchased
easily and is delicious when baked; the fillings can be varied
endlessly. This particular custardlike filling, prepared from semolina, has a most pleasing texture (chewy, not too soft, melts in
your mouth) and is very delicately flavored. It is, needless to say,
highly caloric and difficult to resist.*

KAKAVIA (SERVES 8)

 4 medium onions, sliced very thin
 5 carrots, sliced very thin
 1 head celery, sliced very thin
10 cups water
   juice of 10 lemons
¼ cup oil

4 to 5 pounds sea bass (may also use porgy and perch)
  salt
5 egg yolks

Boil vegetables in water until they are very soft (about 1½ hours).

Beat half the lemon juice with oil. Cut each fish into 4 or 5 large pieces. Salt well and marinate in oil and lemon juice for at least one hour.

Add fish (including marinade) to soup and cook until tender (about 15 minutes). Remove from broth, remove bones and skin, and break fish into small pieces.

Beat egg yolks with the remainder of the lemon juice. Add about 1 cup of broth from soup and blend well. Return this mixture to the soup and mix well. Add fish, stir and let soup sit, covered, for 10 to 15 minutes before serving. Adjust seasoning with salt and pepper as desired.

Optional: Add ⅓ cup of (raw) rice to the soup after it has cooked for 1 hour.

ROAST LEG OF LAMB

1 5-pound leg of lamb
  fresh garlic
  butter
  salt
  pepper
¾ cup olive oil
2 lemons, in thin slices
  juice of one lemon

Wash lamb thoroughly. Pierce meat with knife, making 3 or 4 deep slits on each side. Stuff each slit with a peeled whole garlic clove, some butter, salt and pepper. Sprinkle entire leg with salt and pepper.

Place meat in baking pan. Add ¼ to ½ cup water, plus olive oil. Cover with foil and bake at 250° for 45 minutes. Turn meat over and cover with lemon slices. Add lemon juice to liquid at bottom of pan. Cover with foil again and bake until meat is done (approximately 1 hour).

Before serving, you might want to reduce sauce slightly and thicken with some cornstarch or flour. Serve lamb with potatoes or rice.

GALACTOBOUREKO

1½ quarts milk
 ¼ pound butter
  1 pound semolina
  1 teaspoon vanilla extract
 ¼ teaspoon grated orange rind
 ¼ teaspoon grated lemon rind
 ¼ teaspoon cinnamon
 ½ cup sugar
  3 eggs, beaten

 ¼ pound butter, melted
  1 pound filo

  2 cups water
  2 cups sugar
  3 whole cloves
  1 slice lemon

Bring milk to a boil. Skim.

In a separate pot, melt ¼ pound butter. Over medium heat, stir in semolina and blend well. Slowly add milk and blend. Add vanilla, lemon and orange rind, cinnamon, sugar and eggs. Mix well and heat 15 to 20 minutes, stirring occasionally. Let cool.

Butter a 9×13-inch baking dish. Lay out half the filo and brush generously with melted butter. Spread semolina filling over this and top with remaining filo. Brush again with butter and bake 45 to 60 minutes at 250°, until top of filo is golden and crisp. Let cool.

Simmer water, sugar, cloves and lemon until thick (about 30 to 45 minutes). Remove cloves and lemon slice. Spread half this syrup over cool galactoboureko. Wait a moment, then spread remainder. Serve.

JACK'S NEST

310 THIRD AVENUE
NEW YORK CITY
260-7110

The white waitress at Jack's Nest carefully asked us if we had ever tried chitterlings before agreeing to bring our order. She urged us to try a small sample before tackling an entire dish of entrails, but we assured her that we knew full well what chitterlings were and that we definitely wanted to have some. Still doubting, she eventually brought the dish—a soft, chewy, slightly piquant stew, only faintly suggestive of its origins and delicious with collards and beans. If you're ready for some real soul food, then we recommend the recipe below, prepared daily at the restaurant.

Located in a rather unlikely neighborhood, Jack's Nest is probably the largest soul food restaurant in New York. It is a busy, professionally run establishment, with three Southern chefs who know their food well and prepare it in the unique "down home" style. Hundreds of pounds of ribs, collards, beans and rice are consumed there each week, and all the preparations are tasty, generous and satisfying. Black Eye Peas, Sweet Potato Pie, Carolina Beef Stew and Chitterlings are representative of the fare, which also includes pig's feet, barbecued ribs and an excellent Southern fried chicken.

CHITTERLINGS (SERVES 5)

5 pounds chitterlings
5 cups water
½ cup vinegar
3 onions, chopped
1 teaspoon salt
½ teaspoon Gravy Master or Kitchen Bouquet
2 tablespoons cornstarch

Wash the meat thoroughly, by alternately soaking and rinsing in cold water. Remove all the fat and dirt. (This process should take 1 to 2 hours.)

Cut the meat into small pieces, approximately 1½ inches long.

Soak meat in 2 cups water for 5 minutes. Add vinegar and soak another 10 to 15 minutes. Drain, and rinse.

In a large pot, combine chitterlings with 3 cups water, onions and salt. Bring to a boil, cover and simmer 2½ to 3 hours. Meat should be quite tender. Season with Kitchen Bouquet and add cornstarch dissolved in cold water. Cook another 5 minutes and serve.

CAROLINA BEEF STEW (SERVES 4)

2 pounds beef chuck, in 1-inch cubes
salt
pepper
onion salt

flour
8 tablespoons bacon fat
4 onions, sliced
1½ cups tomato paste
2½ cups beef consommé
2 cups water
6 potatoes, peeled and diced
4 carrots, sliced
1 or 2 16-ounce packages frozen green peas

Season meat with salt, pepper and onion salt. Dredge with flour and brown in bacon fat.

Place meat, onions, tomato paste, consommé and water in casserole. Cover and cook in 325° oven for 1 hour. Add potatoes and carrots, and cook for another 40 minutes. Add peas and cook a few minutes longer. Beef and vegetables should be tender.

BLACK EYE PEAS (SERVES 8 TO 10)

1 pound dry black-eyed peas
1 pound bacon ends or lean salt pork
1 large onion, sliced
1 red pepper, quartered
  salt
  pepper

Rinse peas. Place in pot and add water to twice the depth of the peas. Cover. Bring to boil and boil for 2 minutes. Remove from heat and let stand for at least 1 hour.

In a separate pot, boil the meat in water to cover for about 30 minutes.

Drain the peas thoroughly and add to the meat. Add onion and red pepper. Cover and simmer until peas are tender (about 1 hour). Adjust seasoning with salt and pepper, and serve.

SWEET POTATO PIE (SERVES 6 TO 8)

2 sweet potatoes, boiled and mashed
1 cup sugar
3 eggs, well beaten
¼ cup melted butter
¾ cup milk
1 teaspoon vanilla extract
1 tablespoon sifted flour
  cinnamon to taste
  nutmeg to taste
1 9-inch unbaked pie shell

Mix first 9 ingredients well. Pour into pie shell and bake at 400° for 35 to 40 minutes, until top is browned.

JAMUNA

202 EIGHTH AVENUE
NEW YORK CITY
929-9776

*These recipes from Jamuna, a modest and quiet neighborhood
Indian restaurant, are good versions of classic favorites. The
pillaw is a basically sweet, multiflavored creation, very easy to
prepare and very easy to eat. It is almost like a dessert, and
nicely offsets the spicy Curry and Vegetable Soup. Once you've
prepared both the Pillaw and the Curry, you should try the
Biriani, which is excellent. This dish takes the principle of the
judicious combination of flavors a few steps further.*

*The use of spices in Indian cooking is perhaps more intricate
and refined than in any other cuisine; its mastery requires much
care and experience. Some basics can be learned from these
recipes. Note especially the practice of sautéing the spices for a
while to release all their flavor. Always be sure to use fresh ingredients, or your curry will be tasteless.*

VEGETABLE SOUP (SERVES 6 TO 8)

1 pound lentils
1 onion, chopped very fine
1 green pepper, chopped very fine
1 stalk celery, chopped very fine
2 tomatoes, chopped very fine
2 quarts water
¼ teaspoon ground cardamom seed

    5 bay leaves
    2 teaspoons curry powder
 ¼ teaspoon cumin
    4 whole cloves
    1 1-inch cinnamon stick
       juice of ½ lemon
    5 tablespoons tomato paste
    2 teaspoons minced ginger
    3 cloves garlic, minced

Boil lentils with vegetables until lentils are soft (approximately one hour).

Add all other ingredients except garlic and ginger. Stir well and simmer, covered, for another 20 minutes.

Sauté garlic and ginger in hot vegetable oil for a few minutes, just until they become aromatic. Do not brown or burn. Add to soup and simmer another 5 to 10 minutes.

Strain soup through food mill and serve.

PILLAW (SAFFRON RICE) (SERVES 8 TO 10)

    4 cups long-grain rice
 ½ pound butter
 ½ inch ginger root, in very thin strips
    1 small onion, chopped
    3 cloves garlic, in very thin strips
    6 pieces cardamom seed
    1 2-inch cinnamon stick
    6 bay leaves
    7 cloves
 ½ cup raisins
 ½ cup pignola nuts
       salt

4 tablespoons yogurt
saffron

Wash rice well and leave in a strainer for at least 1 hour.

In a large Dutch oven or casserole, heat butter and gently sauté ginger, onion and garlic. Add cardamom, cinnamon, bay leaves, cloves, raisins and nuts. Sauté a minute or two, add rice, salt to taste, then brown for about 10 minutes. Stir in yogurt.

Bring 3 quarts of water to a boil, dissolving several filaments of saffron in the liquid. Pour boiling water over rice and bring to a second boil. Do not leave pot uncovered for more than 5 minutes. Cover and place in 350° oven for 10 minutes. Turn off heat and allow rice to steam for ½ hour. Rice should be fairly dry. If not, remove cover and leave in oven a few minutes longer.

LAMB CURRY (SERVES 8 TO 10)

4 to 5 cloves garlic, minced
½ inch ginger, minced
1 cup vegetable oil
2 pounds onions, chopped
5 bay leaves
1 1½ inch piece of cinnamon
1 teaspoon Tambrin curry powder
1 teaspoon mixed curry
½ teaspoon hot curry
6 cardamom seeds
1 teaspoon cumin seeds
6 cloves
2 teaspoons salt
4 pounds lamb, cubed

Sauté garlic and ginger in oil. When their aroma is released but before they brown, add onions, bay leaves and cinnamon. Sauté for 5 minutes. Add remainder of seasonings. Stir well and sauté for ½ hour, until mixture is very aromatic. Toward the end, raise the heat for a few minutes to brown the mixture lightly.

Add lamb and brown on all sides. Reduce heat, cover and stew gently for at least 1 hour, adding water as necessary. Serve when lamb is tender.

BIRIANI (1 SERVING)

½ onion, sliced
 2 teaspoons butter
½ green pepper, sliced
 2 cloves garlic, minced
 3 or 4 cardamom seeds
    salt
12 to 16 pieces curried meat, in sauce
1½ cups Pillaw
    grated coconut
    sliced tomato

Sauté onion in butter, adding pepper, garlic, cardamom seeds and salt. Cook over high flame for a minute or two. Then add meat and curry sauce and brown for a few minutes. Add rice, stirring well, and cook until sauce is absorbed by rice.

Garnish with grated coconut and tomato slices. Serve.

JEROME CAFETERIA

48 EAST 161ST STREET
BRONX
ME 5-1242

Strategically situated on a busy Bronx corner, the Jerome Cafeteria has been doing a thriving business in blintzes, roast beef and seltzer since 1936. During a typical 24-hour day, some 2,000 customers pass through the cafeteria's turnstiles, choosing from a huge array of hot and cold dishes. They then make their way to a comfortable spot, where they will sit—sometimes for several hours—talking with old friends, reading the newspaper, watching the street action, passing time. The Jerome invites you to make yourself at home. Amid the bustle of people and the clatter of dishes, it's possible to relax and simply be for a while. Large cafeterias like this one seem to be New York's version of Paris' street cafés: cherished places of rest. One by one, however, these havens are disappearing from our streets, caught in the crunch of increasing food prices and rents.

Happily, the Jerome lives on, thanks to the intelligent and sensitive management of owner Harold Rotkin. His staff consists mainly of old-timers; his clientele is a happy mix of old and new. Mr. Rotkin (who was 16 when his father built the Jerome) generously shared three of the cafeteria's most popular recipes with us. Most notable are the Blintzes, Bronx creations renowned even in Brooklyn.

OXTAIL RAGOUT (SERVES 4)

2 large oxtails, cut (between the joints) into 1½-inch pieces
1 onion
2 stalks celery
1 clove garlic
2 tablespoons shortening
1 teaspoon paprika
2 tablespoons tomato paste
  pepper
2 teaspoons salt
½ teaspoon sugar
½ teaspoon MSG
1 tablespoon shortening
1 tablespoon flour
½ cup cold water

Place oxtails in a baking pan with a little bit of water to cover bottom of pan. Bake, stirring once or twice, at 400° for 30 minutes. Drain off fat.

Grind onion, celery and garlic fine and mix well.

Heat 2 tablespoons shortening in a heavy pot. Add vegetables and paprika, and braise over a low flame until mixture is browned. Add tomato paste and stir well.

Add drained oxtails and stir well. Add enough water to cover meat by 1 inch. Bring to a boil, cover and simmer over low flame for 2 hours. Check occasionally to see if water is needed—meat should always be covered with liquid.

Remove from heat and cool. While cooling, season with pepper, salt, sugar and MSG. Allow to cool for 30 minutes. Fat will come to top. This should be skimmed and discarded.

Heat 1 tablespoon shortening in a frying pan. Add flour and

blend well. Add ½ cup cold water and mix well. Bring meat stew to a boil and add this thickening. Boil for 2 minutes longer and serve.

BLINTZES (ABOUT 8 SERVINGS)

LEAVES (18)

8 eggs
2 cups patent flour
3 cups water
  shortening

Beat eggs well, then stir in flour and water. Beat until smooth.
Over medium heat, warm a 7- or 9-inch frying pan. Rub lightly with butter or shortening. Pour in a small amount of batter to cover surface. Immediately remove pan from heat and pour off batter, leaving only a thin layer in the pan. Return to heat and fry for about 20 seconds. Then pass pan, briefly, under broiler to dry out the top. Turn pan upside down and tap leaf onto counter. Repeat process until all batter is used.

FILLING

6 eggs, beaten
2 pounds cottage cheese
3 cups patent flour
2 to 2½ cups sugar
1 cup melted butter
  pinch of salt

Combine all ingredients and mix well.

Place several tablespoons of filling onto each leaf and roll to create a tight oblong packet. To cook, heat ½ inch of oil or shortening in a frying pan. Make sure oil is hot. Add blintzes and cook until golden brown on both sides, turning once. Drain on paper towels and serve hot with sour cream.

HOT RICE PUDDING WITH FRUIT SAUCE (SERVES 6)

4 cups cooked converted rice
6 eggs
1 quart milk
½ cup sugar
   pinch of salt

Drain rice and place in greased baking pan. There should be 1½ to 2 inches of space above the rice.

Beat eggs thoroughly. Beat together remaining ingredients and fold into eggs. Pour mixture over rice.

Place baking pan in a tray of water and bake for 45 minutes in a 300° oven. When a knife stuck into mixture comes out clean, pudding is ready.

FRUIT SAUCE

1 cup canned or fresh fruit salad (if using canned salad, reduce or omit sugar)
¼ cup sugar
1 cup water
   dash of red food coloring
2 tablespoons cornstarch dissolved in ¼ cup cold water

Combine all ingredients except cornstarch. Bring to a boil. Add cornstarch mixture, stir well and serve hot over rice pudding.

LESHKO'S

111 AVENUE A
NEW YORK CITY
477-9633

Leshko's is one of those plain-looking luncheonettes, to be found all over the city, masking a unique and personal restaurant operation. Actually a Polish-Ukrainian restaurant noted for its Pirogi, Leshko's is graced with the cooking of Mrs. Leshko, a Polish immigrant who 20 years ago opened the restaurant with her husband. Having survived the many cultural changes of the neighborhood, Leshko's continues to serve its community as an unpretentious and relaxed place to get high-quality nourishment at low prices.

Pirogi—meat-, cheese- or potato-filled dumplings—are in that interesting cross-cultural category of filled dough preparations. Almost every ethnic group seems to have one or two specialties of this sort—ravioli, empanadas, samosa, spanakotiropita, etc. Despite the efforts involved, these are especially rewarding dishes to make. Mrs. Leshko's Pirogi are unexcelled, and you should try all the varieties described below. Getting the dough precisely right may be a bit tricky, but Mrs. Leshko insists that practice, not proportions, makes perfect.

CABBAGE SOUP (SERVES 8 TO 10)

1 medium green cabbage, shredded
2 medium onions, chopped
3 ripe tomatoes, chopped
2 tablespoons sauerkraut
  beef stock or water
3 tablespoons tomato purée
1 teaspoon salt
¼ teaspoon pepper
1 onion, sliced
3 tablespoons vegetable oil
3 tablespoons flour

Place cabbage, onions, tomatoes and sauerkraut in large pot. Cover with stock or water, bring to a boil, cover and simmer for at least 2 hours.

Add purée and salt and pepper. Mix well and simmer another hour.

Just before soup is ready to serve, sauté sliced onion in oil. When golden, add flour to form a paste. Mix in a small amount of water to form a creamy sauce, and stir this into soup. Let simmer a few minutes longer.

PIROGI

DOUGH (MAKES ABOUT 6 DOZEN PIROGI)

2½ pounds flour, sifted
1 egg
2½ to 3 cups lukewarm water

Mix flour with egg, and slowly add water, mixing well until flour holds together as a soft dough. Turn onto floured board and knead for at least 5 minutes, until dough is smooth and does not stick. Add flour as necessary. Break dough into pieces and roll out until about ⅛ inch thick. Using a coffee can, cut into 4-inch circles.

Place a heaping tablespoon of filling in center of each circle. Fold over to form a half-moon and pinch edges. (Dip fingers in water to facilitate this.) Drop pirogi into salted, boiling water. Stir. When pirogi rise, remove and coat with vegetable oil. May be stored and fried when desired.

POTATO FILLING (FOR ABOUT 1½ DOZEN PIROGI)

1 pound potatoes, boiled
2 tablespoons butter
2 tablespoons milk
  salt
1 pound farmer cheese, crumbled
1 large onion, chopped and sautéed in butter until golden

Mash potatoes with butter and milk. Season with salt. Let cool. Add farmer cheese and onions and mix, but do not blend completely; farmer cheese should remain in small pieces. Season with salt and pepper if desired.

CHEESE FILLING (FOR ABOUT 1½ DOZEN PIROGI)

1 pound dry farmer cheese
2 or 3 eggs
½ cup sugar (or more, to taste)
¼ cup farina, if desired

Blend all ingredients until creamy.

BEEF FILLING (FOR ABOUT 3 DOZEN PIROGI)

2 pounds beef
2 stalks celery, chopped
2 carrots, sliced
2 onions, chopped
   handful parsley, chopped
1 egg
   salt
   pepper

Boil beef with vegetables until tender. Drain and grind with vegetables. Add egg and mix well. Season to taste with salt and pepper.

APPLE NOODLE PUDDING (SERVES 16)

1 pound fine noodles
4 pounds apples, peeled and sliced
7 eggs, beaten
¼ pound butter, melted
4 teaspoons cinnamon

Boil noodles for 8 minutes. Drain and rinse.

Combine noodles, apples, eggs, butter and cinnamon. Mix well. Spread in buttered baking dishes (two 9×13-inch pans) and bake at 350° for 45 to 60 minutes, until top is brown and apples have "melted."

MESON FLAMENCO

207 WEST 14TH STREET
NEW YORK CITY
243-9205

At Meson Flamenco the fare is purely Spanish—as distinct from the Spanish-influenced food served in New York's numerous Latin-American restaurants. The "true" Spanish style is different from its offshoots, which have blended classical Spanish with native American elements.

Owner and chef Rafael Garcia urged us to point out that the Galician bean soup below has no peppers, onions or garlic, ingredients generally assumed to be the sine qua non of Spanish cuisine. Mr. Garcia also explained that "paella" is a generic term, applicable to anything prepared in the special paella pot. Beef stew cooked in such a pot could legitimately be called paella. But Mr. Garcia went on to say that he offers a "true" paella at Meson Flamenco. We leave the analysis of such questions to others, simply noting that the Paella recipe presented here results in a delicious meal.

GALICIAN BEAN SOUP (SERVES 8)

1   pound Great Northern beans
½   pound chorizos
¼   pound corned spareribs
¼   pound beef (chuck)
¼   pound smoked ham
¼   pound pork belly

3 ounces unto
¼ pound potatoes, peeled and diced
½ pound turnip greens, chopped

Rinse beans and meat. Place beans in pot and cover with water three times as deep as the beans. Add meat and unto. Bring to a boil, cover and simmer 1¼ hours. Remove different pieces of meat as they become tender. During last 20 minutes, add potatoes and greens. Salt to taste. Serve meat separately or combined with the soup.

PAELLA (SERVES 4)

4 tablespoons olive oil
1 2½-pound frying chicken, cut into serving pieces
¼ pound lean pork, sliced
¼ pound squid, sliced
½ cup string beans
½ onion, chopped
1 green pepper, chopped
½ cup large lima beans
1 artichoke heart, quartered
3 cloves garlic, minced
¼ teaspoon paprika
1 tomato, chopped
3 to 4 cups water or stock
   pinch saffron
1½ to 2 cups Uncle Ben's rice
8 clams, cleaned
12 mussels, cleaned
¼ pound shrimp
1 pound lobster (2 tails or 1 whole lobster, split)

Heat oil in a large, flat pan. Add chicken and pork, and sauté for 5 minutes. Add squid, string beans, onion, pepper, lima beans and artichoke. Sauté for several minutes. Add garlic and sauté another 5 minutes. Add paprika and tomato. Stir and sauté another 5 minutes.

Now add water or stock, and bring to a boil, dissolving some saffron in the liquid. Add rice and stir well.

Continue simmering gently as you arrange the shellfish. Bury the clams horizontally in the rice. Stand the mussels up in the rice, bottom ends down. Arrange the shrimp and the lobster on top of the rice. Cover immediately, place in a moderate oven (350° to 400°) and heat for no longer than 20 minutes, until all liquid is absorbed. Remove from oven. Sprinkle with white wine, and garnish with peas, pimentos, parsley and lemon slices.

MEXIFROST SPECIALTIES CO., INC.

220 WEST 13TH STREET
NEW YORK CITY
CH 3-0922

Lucy and Gonzalo Armendariz, the attractive and friendly owners of Mexifrost, have taken great pains to make their little restaurant on West 13th Street a comfortable place to enjoy authentic Mexican and Latin-American foods. The decor is simple and unobtrusive, the small room uncluttered and airy, the food excellently prepared and attractively presented.

The basic repertoire of Mexican food—tacos, enchiladas, tamales, tostadas—is supplemented at Mexifrost by some lesser-known specialties, including the unique Ceviche and Yapingachos. The cook, who recently spent a month studying cooking in Mexico, has a sure and light hand with all these dishes. Everything is prepared fresh daily, including the tortillas, which are manufactured on the premises as part of the Armendariz Mexican-specialties operation.

CEVICHE (6 SERVINGS)

```
 3  cans black clams
    juice of 2 or 3 lemons
½  teaspoon salt
 1  onion, sliced very thin
 1  tomato, chopped
 1  sprig coriander, chopped
 5  or 6 drops Tabasco
    olive oil
```

Marinate clams in lemon juice with salt and onion. Leave in juice for at least 2 hours at room temperature.

Dress with tomato, coriander, Tabasco and olive oil. Serve with tortilla chips and beer.

YAPINGACHOS (SERVES 4 TO 6)

"From the Andes mountains of Ecuador, potatoes filled with cheese and pan-fried to a crisp delight. Topped with a sauce made centuries ago by the Incas."

PANCAKES

    3 pounds Idaho potatoes
    2 tablespoons butter
    1 tablespoon prepared achiote
       salt
       white pepper
1½ to 2 pounds Muenster or mozzarella cheese, coarsely grated

SAUCE

    2 tablespoons butter
    ½ onion, chopped fine
    ¼ cup milk
    1 teaspoon prepared achiote
    2 tablespoons smooth peanut butter

Peel potatoes and boil for about 20 minutes. Don't let them get too soft. Drain and mash with butter, achiote and salt and pepper to taste.

Shape potato mixture into small balls. Flatten and place some cheese in center. Then fold up edges and flatten again, so that you are left with a small, cheese-filled potato pancake. The idea is to get as much cheese surrounded by as little potato as possible. Once you have prepared the pancakes, refrigerate them until you are ready to serve. They can be kept refrigerated, covered with a damp cloth, for as long as 5 days.

To prepare the ancient Inca sauce, heat butter in a saucepan. Add onions and gently sauté until they are translucent. *Do not brown!* Now add milk and achiote, and bring to a boil. Add peanut butter and stir well. Adjust thickness of sauce by adding more peanut butter or milk. Add salt to taste.

To serve, pan-fry the pancakes in lightly oiled pan. Brown slowly on both sides, so that cheese will melt thoroughly. Place on platter and cover each with a spoonful of sauce. Now cover each pancake with a fried egg and pour more sauce over it. Garnish with slices of avocado, lettuce, tomatoes and fried plantain or bananas.

ENCHILADAS SUIZAS (SERVES 4 TO 6)

 1 12-ounce can tomatillos verdes
 2 tablespoons chopped fresh coriander
 1 green pepper, chopped
 2 cloves garlic, chopped
 ½ teaspoon salt
 ⅛ teaspoon pepper

 2 to 3 tablespoons olive oil
 2 medium onions, chopped
 2 green peppers, chopped
 2 tomatoes, chopped
 2½ cups diced cooked chicken

2 teaspoons or more hot chili powder
salt

12 tortillas

2 cups sour cream

To make green sauce, combine tomatillos verdes, cilantro, green pepper, garlic, salt and pepper in blender. Blend until smooth. Chill.

In a large skillet, heat oil and sauté onions and peppers until onions are golden. Add tomatoes and sauté a few minutes longer. Now add chicken and chili powder and sauté another 5 minutes, mixing well. Adjust seasoning.

Place a few tablespoons of chicken mixture in a strip in center of each tortilla. Roll tortilla around filling and place in baking dish. Repeat until you have filled all the tortillas.

Whip sour cream until light. Pour cold green sauce over enchiladas and top with sour cream. Broil under flame for 5 minutes.

(For a spicier enchilada, add some whole jalapeño peppers or their packing sauce to the green sauce.)

MONDONGO (SERVES 8 TO 12)

1 pound dried chick peas
3 pounds honeycomb tripe
½ onion, chopped
3 pig's feet (fresh), cut into small pieces
1 tablespoon cumin
1 teaspoon Tabasco
1 teaspoon salt
1 teaspoon white pepper
prepared achiote

3 chorizos, sliced
1 pound smoked ham, cubed
2 pounds potatoes, peeled and cut into quarters

Soak chick peas overnight. Cut tripe into 2-inch pieces.

Cover tripe with water and boil for a few minutes, then drain all liquid. Cover again with cold water, add onion and chick peas, and simmer, covered, for 1 hour. (Water should be 4 times as deep as tripe and peas.)

Add pig's feet, cumin, Tabasco, salt, pepper and some achiote for color. Continue simmering. After another hour, add chorizos and ham. After another ½ hour, check tripe and chick peas. If tender, add potatoes and cook until potatoes are soft. Otherwise, continue cooking until tender, then add potatoes. Total cooking time should be about 3½ hours. Throughout the cooking, check water level intermittently and replenish if stew begins to dry out.

MI TIERRA

668 AMSTERDAM AVENUE
NEW YORK CITY
787-9593

Before venturing into Mi Tierra, located in the heart of the Latin Upper West Side, you might want to brush up on your Spanish. There's little English spoken in the tiny, dark, crowded room, always saturated with heavy cooking smells from the minuscule open kitchen and usually rocking to a distinct Latin beat from the jukebox. The menu here is primarily Mexican—enchiladas, tacos, Chalupas, refried beans, etc.—and features generous, filling portions at extremely low prices. Everything, except for an occasional stew, is prepared to order by the one Dominican cook. She is a beautiful woman, and her facility at the stove is a remarkable sight. None of her specialties are easy to prepare at home, since they all involve numerous operations of boiling, chopping, grating, slicing, deep frying, sautéing. . . . But if you have the time and are feeling adventurous, the procedures are guaranteed to instantly transport you to Mexico. Be prepared to use all your pots and lots of oil and heat, and to generate aromas that all your neighbors will notice. Tie back your hair, roll up your sleeves and enlist some assistants if you can.

CHALUPAS DE POLLO (SERVES 6)

2 cups dry black beans
3 to 4 pounds chicken
  olive oil
4 medium onions, coarsely chopped
½ teaspoon garlic powder
  salt
  pepper
2 tablespoons lard
1 dozen tortillas
6 ripe bananas
1 head lettuce, shredded
12 slices tomato
½ pound cheddar or American cheese, grated

Soak beans overnight. Simmer for 2½ hours, or just until tender.

Clean chicken and remove meat from bones, cutting into small strips, about ¼ × 1 inch.

Heat 2 tablespoons olive oil in large skillet and add chicken, onion, garlic powder and salt and pepper to taste. Sauté over medium-high heat until chicken is thoroughly cooked and onions are browned (about 15 minutes).

In another skillet, heat lard and sauté cooked, drained beans for 10 minutes, seasoning with salt and pepper.

Heat olive oil in heavy pot and deep-fry tortillas until they are golden and crisp. Drain on paper towels. Cut bananas into 1-inch diagonal slices and fry in the same oil.

To serve: Place 2 tortillas on each plate. Spread a few table-spoons of the fried beans on each tortilla. Cover this with the chicken-and-onion mixture, then with a mound of lettuce, next a tomato slice, then finally with a generous handful of grated cheese. Garnish each plate with banana slices.

VENEZUELAN PAVEJÓN (SERVES 4 TO 6)

1 cup black beans
1 onion, chopped
2 cloves garlic, minced
  olive oil
2 tablespoons tomato paste
1 tablespoon vinegar
  salt
2 pounds beef flank
1 green pepper, chopped
1 onion, chopped
1 clove garlic, minced
4 bananas
2 cups cooked rice

Soak beans overnight, then simmer gently for about 2 hours.

Sauté 1 chopped onion and 2 minced cloves of garlic in 1 tablespoon olive oil; add tomato paste, vinegar and salt to taste. Add to beans and simmer another hour.

Boil beef until tender (2 to 3 hours). Remove from water and shred into thin filaments.

Sauté pepper and remaining onion and garlic in 2 tablespoons olive oil. Add shredded beef and brown.

Deep-fry bananas, sliced on diagonal, in very hot olive oil.

To serve, spoon some beans, rice and beef onto each plate. Surround with fried bananas and fresh tomato wedges.

DOMINICAN SANCOCHO (SERVES 6 TO 8)

2 onions, chopped
2 cloves garlic, minced
   lemon juice
   salt
   few sprigs cilantro
4 tablespoons lard
1 pound beef, cubed
1 pound pork, cubed
1 pound chicken, cubed
1 banana, sliced
1 cup cubed yuca
1 cup cubed pumpkin
1 cup cubed ñame
1 cup cubed yautía
5 cups water
   pepper

In a blender, combine onions, garlic, 3 tablespoons lemon juice, 2 teaspoons salt and cilantro. Blend well. Coat meat with this mixture and marinate at room temperature for at least one hour.

In large saucepan, heat lard and brown meat well. Add vegetables. Cover with water, bring to boil and simmer, covered, 30 to 45 minutes. Season with more lemon juice, salt and pepper to taste. Serve with rice and hot sauce.

MOLFETAS

307 WEST 47TH STREET
NEW YORK CITY
586-9278

*Steam tables and cafeteria-style service are usually a sign of
bland, overcooked food, with nothing to recommend it but its
availability and price. Not so at Molfetas, where the restaurant's
Greek specialties are attractively displayed on steam tables be-
hind a glass counter. Instead of consulting a menu, you can take
a look at the preparations of the day, perhaps stopping to ask
the countermen for recommendations and descriptions. The custom is a common one in Greece and throughout the Middle East,
and adds to the relaxed atmosphere of this comfortably func-
tional restaurant.*

*Nick Triantafillo, head chef at Molfetas for nearly twenty
years and currently a part owner, was delighted to share his
recipes with us. Once again, note that Greek dishes cannot be
made effortlessly, so when making Mousaka at home, leave yourself plenty of time and enjoy the rather sensuous process of putting together this subtle but filling dish. The string bean recipe
results in a characteristically Greek, robust and tasty stew—a far
cry from more common Western versions of the beans. Definitely
simpler to make than the Mousaka, this basic stew may be further
enhanced by the addition of lamb chunks. You may also substitute okra for the beans, for a more exotic version of the dish.*

GREEK STRING BEANS (SERVES 6 TO 8)

```
 3  or 4 medium onions, sliced
 3  tablespoons olive oil
10  ounces tomato paste
 2  cloves garlic, minced
    handful of fresh dill, coarsely chopped
    bunch parsley, coarsely chopped
 1  teaspoon salt
¼  teaspoon black pepper
¾  cup water
 2  pounds string beans, washed and cut into 4-inch pieces
 4  large tomatoes, quartered
```

Sauté onions in 1 tablespoon olive oil until golden.

Add tomato paste, garlic, dill, parsley, salt, pepper and ¾ cup water to form a thick sauce. Simmer gently, stirring occasionally, for about 10 minutes.

Add beans, tomatoes, half as much water and 2 tablespoons olive oil. Cover and simmer gently 1½ to 2 hours, stirring occasionally.

MOUSAKA (SERVES 6 TO 8)

```
 2  or 3 large eggplants
    salt
 2  onions, sliced
    olive oil
```

1½ to 2 pounds ground or minced lamb
  3 ounces tomato paste
  ½ cup water
    pepper
  6 tablespoons butter
  6 tablespoons flour
  4 eggs
  2 cups milk
  4 tablespoons grated Parmesan cheese

Wash eggplants and cut into ½-inch slices. Place in a colander and salt thoroughly. Let sit at least 20 minutes, press out the water and rinse thoroughly. Pat dry with towels.

Sauté onions in 1 tablespoon olive oil. Add meat and cook over medium-high heat until browned. Add tomato paste, water, salt and pepper, and simmer 15 to 20 minutes.

Deep-fry eggplant slices in very hot olive oil just until slices are golden brown. This should take no more than 2 or 3 minutes for each slice—if it takes any longer your oil is not hot enough and the eggplant will absorb too much of it. Drain the fried slices on paper towels.

In a large baking dish, put down a layer of closely packed eggplant slices. Cover this with the meat sauce, then with a second layer of eggplant.

Melt butter over low heat. Add flour and blend well until a bubbly paste is formed. Away from heat, blend in eggs and milk, stirring constantly. Simmer a few minutes and add 2 or 3 tablespoons grated Parmesan. Continue to cook over low heat, stirring constantly, until sauce thickens.

Pour this sauce over the eggplant and sprinkle with Parmesan.

Bake in 350° oven for ½ hour. The crust should be brown and crisp, with a creamy layer of custard topping the layers of meat and eggplant.

FLOGERA

2 tablespoons flour
2 cups milk
2 egg yolks, beaten
1 tablespoon butter
2 teaspoons vanilla

½ pound filo
¼ pound butter, melted

2 cups sugar
1 cup water

Blend flour with milk. Place in saucepan and slowly bring to a boil, stirring constantly. Continue simmering for 5 minutes after milk has boiled.

Remove about ½ cup of milk and beat with egg yolks. Return this to the saucepan and heat until boiling again, stirring constantly. Just before removing from heat, stir in butter and vanilla. Let cool.

Butter an 8×8-inch baking dish. Lay out 2 leaves of filo, folding edges under to fit pan. Be sure to alternate sides when you are folding, to avoid an uneven buildup of layers. Brush with melted butter. Lay out another 2 leaves and brush again with butter. Continue until you have used half the filo. Spread custard over filo, then top with remaining leaves, using the same procedure as before. Brush top generously with butter. Bake for about 45 minutes at 300°, until filo is golden and crisp.

While flogera is baking, simmer sugar and water until thick. Let cool. Spread over hot flogera. Cool, cut into slices and serve.

Flogera may also be prepared by rolling 2 or 3 leaves of filo around the custard, to form narrow cylinders. Fold leaves in half lengthwise. Brush with melted butter. Spread a layer of custard along near edge and gently roll dough around filling. Bake in buttered baking dish, as above. Cooking time will be slightly shorter.

MONYA'S

For a short time, there was an outstanding health-foods restaurant. Monya kept the place spotlessly clean; all the food was freshly prepared and very tasty. The work involved was too demanding for her, so Monya left the business—though not before sharing one excellent recipe with us. Garbanzo-Bulgur Casserole is a delicious and economical dish, based on the unique grain product bulgur, which has been slowly gaining popularity here. An excellent substitute for rice, bulgur has a nutty, earthy flavor which goes well with any number of seasonings.

GARBANZO-BULGUR CASSEROLE (SERVES 4)

    1 cup garbanzos (dried chick peas)
    3 tablespoons vegetable oil
    ¾ cup chopped onion
    ¾ cup chopped celery
    ¾ cup chopped green pepper
    1 cup coarse bulgur
    1 teaspoon salt
    2 to 4 ounces tomato sauce or juice

Soak garbanzos overnight. Drain, rinse and place in pot. Cover with water, 1½ inches higher than the beans. Bring to a boil, cover and simmer 3 to 4 hours.

Heat oil in large casserole. Sauté onions, celery and green pepper until onions are golden. Add rinsed bulgur, and brown for 5 or 10 minutes. Now pour about 3 cups of boiling water over the vegetables and bulgur (For an improvement in flavor, you may use the water in which the chick peas have been boiling). Add salt and tomato sauce, and cover. Simmer about 20 minutes until water is absorbed. Add drained, cooked garbanzos and cook a few minutes longer. Add more tomato sauce if desired.

NEAR EAST

138 COURT STREET
BROOKLYN
624-9257

A modestly decorated open room provides the graceful setting for excellent Arabic food at the Near East in Brooklyn. The dishes are prepared under the careful supervision of Kaid Almontaser, whose brother Mosad serves as waiter. Their uncle Mohammed is the proprietor of the nearby Atlantic House. Originally from Yemen, the Almontaser family has evidently succeeded in making a happy and prosperous transition to life in New York.

The afternoon we visited the restaurant, several men were sitting in the kitchen, carefully trimming and chopping large quantities of lamb for Saba Glaba. They were relaxed and peaceful at their work, withdrawn into private silences yet sharing in their simple task with quiet pleasure. Friends and neighboring businessmen dropped in casually to say hello and wish a good day to Mosad and Kaid; a few lingered to talk with us over coffee. The place seemed to have been functioning in this quietly affectionate manner for all eternity; time slipped away as we sat in the fading light and talked about the way the world is. From our vantage point in that happy room, the view was good.

SABA GLABA (SERVES 2 TO 4)

1 pound lean lamb, cut into ½-inch cubes
2 onions, chopped
1 green pepper, chopped
2 cloves garlic, minced

Mosad Almontaser poses outside his restaurant on Court Street.

1 teaspoon cumin
1 teaspoon allspice
¼ teaspoon curry
1 teaspoon salt
¼ teaspoon pepper
  Tomato Sauce (see below)

Sauté lamb with onion, pepper, garlic and dry seasonings over a medium flame, stirring occasionally, for 15 minutes. Add Tomato Sauce and simmer, uncovered, for 20 minutes.

TOMATO SAUCE

1 large onion, chopped
1 green pepper, chopped
3 cloves garlic, chopped
3 tablespoons olive oil
2 6-ounce cans tomato paste
4 cups water and/or chicken broth
¼ to ½ teaspoon curry
1 teaspoon cumin
1 tablespoon oregano
2 bay leaves
2 tablespoons flour
1 tablespoon oil

Sauté onion, pepper and garlic in 3 tablespoons olive oil until onions are golden. Add tomato paste, broth and seasonings. Simmer uncovered, stirring occasionally, for 2 hours.

Brown flour in 1 tablespoon oil and add to sauce, stirring in well.

LAMB AND OKRA STEW (SERVES 4)

4 onions, chopped
½ head garlic, minced
6 tablespoons olive oil
1½ pounds lamb shank in 1-inch cubes
1 6-ounce can tomato paste
1 tablespoon thyme
2 teaspoons salt
½ teaspoon pepper
1 cup chicken broth
½ pound okra

Sauté onions and garlic in olive oil. Add lamb and brown. Add tomato paste, seasonings and broth. Simmer, covered, for 45 minutes, until meat is nearly done. Add okra and simmer another 15 minutes.

BABA GHANOUJ

1 small eggplant
2 tablespoons tahini
1 tablespoon lemon juice
½ teaspoon salt
¼ teaspoon pepper
1 tablespoon chopped fresh dill
1 clove garlic, minced

Bake eggplant at 400° until soft. Let cool and remove pulp. Grind and combine with other ingredients. Blend well. Chill and serve topped with olive oil.

KAMMER AL-DIN (SERVES 12)

2 quarts water
½ pound amar din
1 cup sugar
½ teaspoon cardamom seed
½ cup cornstarch dissolved in 1 cup cold water

Bring water, amar din, sugar and cardamom seed to a boil. Stir in dissolved cornstarch. Simmer, covered, for 20 minutes. Pour into a mold.

Let cool, refrigerate and serve.

THE NEW KOREA

9 EAST 40TH STREET
NEW YORK CITY
MU 3-7775

Watching an Oriental chef at work is both exhilarating and humbling. Sung Jin Hong, Korean chef for 20 years and owner of The New Korea for 2, had us in open-mouthed amazement when he demonstrated the preparation of the two dishes below. He sliced the vegetables and set them to boil faster than we could note the ingredients; he cut the meat and fish and coated them with batter and was frying them before we had a chance to glance back at the vegetables. It all looked so easy. . . .

Interested amateurs are invited to visit Mr. Hong in his kitchen weekdays between 3 and 5 P.M.

SAM HAP CHO (SERVES 2)

¼ cup thinly sliced squash
¼ cup thinly sliced carrot
¼ cup thinly sliced onion
¼ green pepper, in 1-inch-square pieces
10 ginkgo nuts (canned)
4 white mushrooms, sliced
handful cloud ears, sliced
1 ¼-inch slice of fish cake (canned, available in Chinatown)
½ cup rice vinegar
¼ cup rice wine (Mirin)
2 tablespoons soy sauce
1 teaspoon salt
1 cup sugar

3 tablespoons flour
3 tablespoons cornstarch
2 eggs
½ cup cubed beef
4 large shrimp, flattened and sliced
1 medium abalone, in thin slices
  oil for deep frying
2 tablespoons cornstarch dissolved in ¼ cup cold water

Combine vegetables and fish cake with vinegar, wine, soy sauce, salt and sugar. Place in saucepan and bring to boil. Simmer, uncovered, 10 to 15 minutes.

Combine flour, cornstarch and eggs to form light batter. Coat beef, shrimp and abalone with batter and deep-fry (about 5 minutes) until golden. Drain and arrange on serving plate.

Thicken vegetable sauce with dissolved cornstarch. Heat a few minutes longer and pour over meat and fish. Serve.

BUL GO KI (SERVES 2)

1 pound flank steak, sliced as thin as possible, then pounded
½ cup scallions, cut in thin strips
1 tablespoon sugar
½ teaspoon black pepper
1 tablespoon soy sauce
1 teaspoon garlic powder
2 tablespoons sesame oil
½ cup beef stock
1 teaspoon rice wine (Mirin)

Combine all ingredients and allow meat to marinate, uncovered, at room temperature for at least one hour.

Broil beef over high heat, turning slices of meat so that they cook through thoroughly, and serve with a mixture of rice vinegar and soy sauce for dunking.

OLÉ

434 SECOND AVENUE
NEW YORK CITY
725-1953

Tony and Joseph Legares, respectively chef and owner of Olé, are happily carrying on a tradition begun by their grandfather, who once ran a Spanish restaurant on West 11th Street. Their restaurant serves authentic Spanish food in a nondescript American room, to the accompaniment of Spanish guitar every evening. Tony, who began cooking when he was 16, brings a fine and imaginative hand to his preparations, which range from traditional standards to personal inventions—note the delicious and perhaps unprecedented Chicken Villaroy.

CALDO GALLEGO (SERVES 6 TO 8)

1 cup white navy beans
1 pound salted pork ribs (spareribs)
¼ pound salted lard
4 quarts water
1 head cabbage, cut into pieces
4 potatoes, quartered
3 or 4 chorizos, cut into quarters

Soak beans overnight. Soak spareribs and lard overnight, then rinse well to remove salt. Cook beans until tender.

Bring spareribs and lard to boil in 4 quarts water and simmer for 1½ hours, covered, until meat is tender.

Add cabbage. After 10 minutes, add potatoes, drained beans and chorizos. Cook another 20 minutes and season with salt and pepper.

SHRIMP IN GARLIC SAUCE (SERVES 4)

1 pound shrimp, shelled and deveined
2 lemons
½ cup chopped parsley
  salt
  pepper
5 ounces olive oil
3 cloves garlic, minced
½ cup white wine
  Mushroom Sauce (see below)

Place cleaned shrimp in dish. Squeeze fresh lemon juice over them and season with parsley, salt and pepper.

Heat olive oil and brown garlic. Add shrimp and sauté until nearly done. Add white wine and Mushroom Sauce. Simmer a few minutes longer, then serve over rice.

MUSHROOM SAUCE

½ pound sliced mushrooms
2 tablespoons butter
4 tablespoons cornstarch or flour
1 cup beef stock
¼ cup sherry

Sauté mushrooms in butter. Add cornstarch or flour and blend well. Add beef stock and sherry and stir in well. Simmer 5 to 10 minutes to create a thick sauce.

CHICKEN VILLAROY (SERVES 4)

2 whole chicken breasts
1 cup white sauce
¼ cup flour
2 eggs, beaten
1 cup plain bread crumbs
½ cup chopped parsley
  vegetable oil for deep frying

Boil chicken breasts in salted water until tender (about 45 minutes). Remove skin and bones, and split breasts. (To make it easier but more expensive, you can buy professionally skinned and boned chicken.)

Dip breasts in white sauce, making sure to coat well, and chill for several hours.

When ready to serve, dip breasts into flour, then into eggs, then finally into bread crumbs and parsley. Deep-fry in vegetable oil until golden and serve.

YELLOW RICE (SERVES 4 TO 6)

2 onions, chopped
3 to 5 cloves garlic, chopped
1 or 2 green peppers, chopped
4 tablespoons olive oil
1 cup rice
  pinch of saffron
2 cups chicken stock

In a large casserole, sauté onions, garlic and peppers in oil until onions are golden. Add rinsed rice and brown, stirring well.

Dissolve saffron in hot chicken stock and pour into the casserole. Bring to a boil, stir, cover and place in a 325° oven for 20 minutes.

The exact recipe for Olé's excellent chicken stock is not to be had, but we did learn that the following ingredients are used to prepare this savory broth:

chicken bones and wings
shell steak bones
onions
carrots
celery
tomatoes
eggshells
shrimp shells
peppers
garlic
salt
fish heads

Everything should be boiled together for at least 3 hours, and with a little experimentation you should be able to come up with a reasonably tasty facsimile.

162 SPRING STREET

NEW YORK CITY
431-7637

Jimmy Halpin is in his early 20s. He's been working as a chef since he was 14, beginning in his hometown near Dublin, working his way through Ireland, then finally in Dublin for a year. Two years in Bermuda were the next stop on his culinary journey, which ultimately brought him to New York and the comfortable elegance of 162 Spring Street. There the owners have given him free rein in the kitchen, where Jimmy supervises a small, cheerful staff and produces excellent, often original versions of classic Continental and American dishes: quiche Lorraine, ratatouille, omelets, carbonnade provençale . . . roast chicken, pork chops, cheeseburgers. Distinguished is perhaps the best word to describe his high-quality preparations, obviously made with great care and appreciatively consumed by the patrons of this uniquely designed restaurant/haven in SoHo.

VEAL CURRY (SERVES 4 TO 6)

3 pounds veal necks in 1-inch cubes
¼ pound white raisins
2 tablespoons Imperial curry
2 chopped apples
1 quart orange juice
1 pint chicken stock
1 quart water
  salt, pepper to taste

½ pound margarine
¾ cup flour

Combine all ingredients except flour and margarine in large, heavy pot. Simmer gently, uncovered, for 30 minutes.

Prepare roux from margarine and flour. Add to veal stew and mix well. Simmer slowly another 30 to 40 minutes, until veal is tender. Serve with sliced bananas and freshly shredded coconut.

This dish may also be made with leftover lamb. Cook all ingredients except lamb, then add meat about 10 minutes before cooking is completed.

POTAGE PARISIENNE (SERVES 4)

2 leeks, diced
1 onion, diced
¼ pound margarine
1 quart chicken stock
½ cup white wine
3 bay leaves
3 large potatoes, diced
  salt
  pepper
  parsley

Sauté leeks and onions in margarine, but do not brown. Add stock, wine, bay leaves and potatoes. Bring to boil and simmer, covered, for one hour. Add salt and pepper to taste, and garnish with freshly chopped parsley.

THE PARADOX

The Paradox, alas, is no longer. In its time, it was the macrobiotic restaurant of the East Village—the hippest, friendliest, most comfortable place to eat your daily ration of brown rice and vegetables and discuss the events of the day with your familiars in freakiness.

The macrobiotic craze has faded into obscurity, its leaders dispersed, its followers bored. But the virtues of brown rice and simply cooked vegetables remain unchanged . . . the food is cheap, easy to prepare and most satisfying to, yes, the body and the soul. The colors and textures are particularly pleasing, the flavors distinctive and slightly addictive. Observing the old macrobiotic edict (with a grain of sesame salt) that you should chew each grain of rice at least 100 times adds to the pleasure of the food.

We're happy to have rescued the Paradox's Tempura recipe from oblivion. The mixture of the different flours creates a light, tasty batter which bears no resemblance to the standard Japanese tempura. It's an easy and economical way to prepare vegetables and fish, properly accompanied by brown rice and seaweed.

TEMPURA BATTER

¼ cup soy flour
¼ cup arrowroot
¼ cup whole-wheat flour
¼ cup sweet rice flour
2 teaspoons corn flour or corn meal

½ teaspoon sea salt
1 to 1¼ cups bubbly spring water

This is the basic tempura batter that was used at the Paradox. Cut vegetables are dipped into the chilled batter and deep-fried in soy oil. The vegetables should also be chilled, and the oil should be at over 350°. Fry just until the batter is browned, drain and serve hot. Vegetables good as tempura include carrots, onions, watercress, cauliflower, celery, squash and corn. Butterfly shrimp and fish are also excellent.

To create the batter, just mix the first 6 ingredients lightly. Add enough spring water to create a thin, creamy mixture, and ignore lumps.

MACROBIOTIC SALAD DRESSING (ENOUGH FOR 3 LARGE SALADS)

1½ cups corn oil
1 medium onion, chopped
  handful parsley or spinach, with stems cut off
¼ lemon (including peel)
½ to 1 teaspoon tamari
½ teaspoon sea salt

Place all ingredients in a blender and blend until creamy. Chill and serve over any salad vegetables. For variety, add any other herbs or greens to this basic mixture.

APPLE CRUNCH (SERVES 6 TO 8)

  4 cups sliced apples
½ to 1 cup currants or raisins
½ to 1 cup chopped nuts
  2 teaspoons cinnamon
  1 teaspoon grated lemon rind
  1 cup rolled oats
⅓ cup sifted whole-wheat flour
½ teaspoon salt
¼ cup oil

Place apples in an oiled, shallow baking dish and sprinkle with currants, nuts, cinnamon and lemon rind.

Combine oats, flour and salt. Add oil, mixing until crumbly.

Sprinkle the crumb mixture over the apples and bake in a 350° oven 30 to 45 minutes, until apples are soft.

PHILIPPINE GARDEN

455 SECOND AVENUE
NEW YORK CITY
MU 4-9625 AND MU 5-5855

At Philippine Garden, the full range of native cuisine is prepared by Mr. Olavario, a chef in the Philippines since 1933 and master of the kitchen here for nearly 20 years. The restaurant is a quiet, tropical-feeling establishment, graced by Philippine waitresses with beautiful, proud faces. They are anxious to please with their food, which, though unfamiliar to American palates, contains some rich surprises.

KILAWIN (SERVES 4)

```
  1  pound pork butt, cut into thin strips ( ¼ × 1½ inches )
  1  pound pork liver, cut into thin strips ( ¼ × 1½ inches )
1½  cups vinegar
  ¼  pound lard
  3  cloves garlic, crushed
  1  teaspoon black pepper
     salt
```

Soak meat in vinegar for a few minutes. Drain and reserve vinegar. Melt lard in skillet. Add meat and brown. Now add vinegar, garlic, pepper and salt to taste. Simmer uncovered for 1 hour, until sauce thickens and meat is very tender.

GINATAN (SERVES 8)

½ pound plantain
½ pound yuca
½ pound yams
½ pound gabi
½ cup water
 1 cup sweet rice flour
 1 cup coconut milk
 2 pounds sugar
 1 cup jackfruit juice
 2 tablespoons cornstarch dissolved in ¼ cup cold water

Dice all vegetables into ½-inch cubes.

Add water to the rice flour and prepare a thick dough. Roll out and cut into ½-inch cubes.

In large pot, bring coconut milk and sugar to a boil. Add vegetables, dough and jackfruit juice. Simmer, covered, for 1 hour. Thicken with dissolved cornstarch. Chill and serve.

PIERRE AU TUNNEL

306 WEST 48TH STREET
NEW YORK CITY
265-9039

*Pierre Pujol is a restaurant proprietor in the classic French man-
ner. A cheerful, cosmopolitan man, he single-handedly does the
marketing each morning for the medium-sized, moderately priced
restaurant which he has been operating for over 25 years. Pierre
au Tunnel (named not in honor of the nearby Lincoln Tunnel,
but in keeping with the long, narrow room decorated with false-
brick archways) is a comfortable, bistro-type place, offering
generous portions of bourgeois French cuisine. M. Pujol is a
member of the Vatel Club, "la plus importante association culi-
naire aux États-Unis," and he has achieved the distinction of
"Commandeur" in the Commanderie des Cordons Bleus. Originally an apprentice chef in France, he personally trained his current chef, Angelo Nieves, 19 years ago, and now cooks only for
pleasure at home. The recipes he shared with us are classic
French favorites—especially the Cassoulet, which is relatively
unknown in New York.*

PÂTÉ MAISON (ABOUT 16 4-OUNCE SERVINGS)

1 pound pork liver
2 pounds lean pork
¾ pound pork fat
4 chicken livers
2 teaspoons salt

¼ teaspoon pepper
¼ teaspoon thyme
½ teaspoon sage
¼ cup muscatel raisins
¾ cup sherry
¼ cup cognac
2 bay leaves

Grind together pork liver, pork, pork fat and chicken livers, using the fine blade of a meat grinder.

Add salt, pepper, thyme, sage, raisins, sherry and cognac. Mix thoroughly and turn into a well-greased 2½-quart earthenware casserole. Top with bay leaves and cover. Bake at 350° for 1½ hours. Uncover and bake 20 minutes longer. Let cool, then remove from casserole, slice and serve well chilled.

MOULES RAVIGOTE (SERVES 2 AS AN APPETIZER)

Cook about 1 pound of mussels in white wine and water (about 5 ounces wine to 8 ounces water). Cook until mussels are open. Chill in refrigerator, leaving mussels in broth.

To make the sauce, start with a basic mayonnaise, adding very finely chopped chives, crushed capers and some ketchup for coloring.

Remove cooled mussels from broth and serve on the half shell, with a piece of lemon in the center to create the appearance of a daisy. Place sauce on top of each mussel and serve.

MOULES MARINIÈRE (SERVES 2)

 3 pounds mussels, cleaned
10 ounces dry white wine
10 ounces water
 1 shallot, chopped very fine
   handful of chives, chopped very fine
½ teaspoon salt
   freshly ground black pepper

Place mussels in a large pot. Add wine, water, shallots, chives
and salt. Grind pepper over top. Cover pot and place over high
flame for about 7 minutes, or until mussels are open. Stir them
occasionally if they do not seem to open immediately. After not
more than 10 minutes, serve. The mussels that are not open are
generally not good and should not be eaten.

BOEUF BOURGIGNON (SERVES 4 TO 6)

 1 cup diced salt pork or bacon
 1 tablespoon fat
 3 pounds bottom round beef, cut into cubes
 1 tablespoon salt
   dash pepper
12 small white onions
 6 medium carrots, quartered
 2 shallots, chopped
 1 clove garlic, crushed

2 tablespoons flour
2 cups red wine
2 cups beef stock
2 stalks celery
3 sprigs parsley
1 bay leaf
  dash thyme
½ pound mushrooms, sliced
2 tablespoons butter or margarine

Cook salt pork and fat until pork is golden brown. Remove pork. Season beef with salt and pepper. Brown well in fat and remove. Brown onions and carrots. Skim off fat, then remove vegetables. Add chopped shallots, crushed garlic and flour. Mix well and cook, stirring, until flour browns. Add red wine, stock, meat and browned vegetables. Add water to cover meat. Tie celery, parsley, bay leaf and thyme in cheesecloth. Add to meat. Cover and simmer over low heat for 2 hours. Sauté mushrooms in butter. Add to stew and serve with boiled potatoes or noodles.

CASSOULET TOULOUSAINE

3 pounds white beans
1 garlic sausage
1 clove garlic, crushed
1 tablespoon salt
  dash of black pepper
1 carrot, chopped
1 onion, chopped
2 cloves
1 faggot made of 2 sprigs parsley, 1 stalk celery, 1 bay leaf
  and some thyme

1 onion, chopped fine
1 tablespoon butter
2 cloves garlic, chopped
3 tomatoes, peeled, seeded and chopped
¼ cup chopped parsley

1 roast duck
2 pounds roast lamb

Soak the beans overnight. Cook until soft with sausage, garlic, salt, pepper, carrot, chopped onion, cloves and faggot. Leave in the saucepan where they will keep warm.

Lightly brown the finely chopped onion in butter in another saucepan. Add the garlic, tomatoes and parsley. Let boil a few minutes. Drain white beans and add to this sauce, reserving sausage. Correct seasoning and add gravy from the roast duck.

Slice the duck, the lamb and the sausage. Place a layer of beans in the bottom of an earthenware casserole. Cover with slices of duck, lamb and sausage. Cover with a layer of beans, and alternate until casserole is full. Sprinkle the top with bread crumbs and a little butter or duck fat, and brown in oven or broiler. Serve very hot.

CHOCOLATE MOUSSE (SERVES 6)

6 ounces semisweet chocolate
1 tablespoon fresh-ground coffee
3 tablespoons butter
6 eggs, separated
½ cup heavy cream
5 tablespoons sugar

Melt the chocolate with the coffee in the upper part of a double boiler over hot—not boiling—water. Add the butter and stir until melted.

Beat the egg yolks until very light. Slowly add the chocolate mixture, beating over hot water until smooth. Cool.

Whip the cream and add the sugar. Then beat the egg whites until very stiff. Fold whipped cream and egg whites into chocolate mixture. Chill and serve.

PIERRE'S FALAFEL

111 COURT STREET
BROOKLYN
TR 5-9137

Pierre Borday and his enterprising family have put falafel on New York's culinary map. Pierre sets up a falafel place, trains help, then sells the business to the new falafel expert. At this writing, the establishment on Court Street is the only one still owned by Pierre.

Pierre's wife, Leona, gave us the following recipes, although she insisted on guarding the secret of the successful falafel. Fool Mudamas is a unique and delicious Arab staple. It is filling, cheap and very easy to make. Chommos and Kibbe are further Arab favorites.

FOOL MUDAMAS (SERVES 2)

1 can small fava beans ("fool mudamas"—Sahadi or Violet
    brand)
4 cloves garlic
  lemon juice
  salt
  pepper
  olive oil
  chopped parsley

Heat beans until liquid begins to boil. Drain.

Mash garlic with beans, adding lemon juice, salt and pepper to taste.

Serve on plate or on pita bread. Top with olive oil and parsley.

CHOMMOS

1 20-ounce can chick peas
½ cup tahini
2 cloves garlic, minced
   lemon juice
   salt
   olive oil
   paprika
   parsley

Heat chick peas and simmer several minutes. Drain and blend in blender for 2 or 3 minutes.

Dilute tahini with some water. Add water slowly and stir until mixture is creamy and white.

Add tahini and garlic to blended chick peas. Add lemon juice and salt to taste. Mix well.

Serve on platter topped with olive oil, paprika and chopped parsley.

KIBBE (SERVES 4 TO 6)

1 cup fine bulgur
2 pounds very lean lamb, finely ground
1 medium onion, grated
   salt
   pepper

1 pound lamb (with some fat), coarsely ground
2 large onions, diced
½ cup pignola nuts
  salt
  nutmeg

Rinse bulgur in cold water. Combine with finely ground lamb and grated onion, and season with salt and pepper. Spread half of this mixture in greased 12×8-inch pan.

In large skillet, sauté coarsely ground lamb, onions and pignola nuts until meat is well browned. Season with salt and nutmeg.

Spread this mixture over the layer of bulgur and lamb. Cover with remainder of bulgur-and-lamb mixture. Brush top with oil or margarine, and cut into diamond-shaped pieces. Bake at 350° for 20 minutes.

PONCE DE LEON

171 EAST 116TH STREET
NEW YORK CITY
348-5580 AND LE 4-9647

The Ponce de Leon is open 364 days a year, closing only on December 24 and early on New Year's Eve. It is a well-loved institution on East 116th Street, providing its patrons with high-quality Latin food (Puerto Rican, Cuban, Spanish) at modest prices in elegant and relaxing surroundings.

Owner Rodrigo Rodriguez began as a waiter in Cuba when he was 15. Since then, he and his brothers have owned and managed several restaurants here and in the Caribbean. Ponce de Leon (originally called the Capri) was opened in 1963; at that time the restaurant boasted 3 stools and 10 tables, with Mr. Rodriguez as chef. The restaurant has greatly expanded since then, including now an upstairs cocktail lounge featuring a "Fountain of Youth." The original small-family feeling has been preserved, however, and the Ponce de Leon is a comforting place to dine.

RICE WITH SQUID AND INK (SERVES 6)

1 cup olive oil
1 medium onion, diced
1 medium green pepper, diced
3 cloves garlic, minced
2 tablespoons salt
1 cup consommé

1 pound rice
3 4-ounce cans squid (cuttlefish) in its own ink

Heat olive oil in a large saucepan. Add onions, peppers, garlic and salt. Sauté until onions are translucent.

Add consommé, rice, squid and ink. Stir well, bring to a boil, cover and simmer 20 to 25 minutes. Serve with Tostones.

TOSTONES (SERVES 6)

5 green plantains
  olive oil for deep frying

Peel plantains and cut into 1-inch slices. Deep-fry in hot oil for 10 minutes. Drain.

Flatten each piece of plantain, using either your palm or a broad cleaver. The "tostones" may be stored under a damp cloth until you are ready to serve. Deep-fry for 5 minutes and drain.

BOLICHE (SERVES 6 TO 8)

1 round roast (eye round)—about 4 pounds
3 or 4 chorizos
4 tablespoons lard or olive oil
3 cloves garlic, minced
2 onions, chopped
1 green pepper, chopped
2 8-ounce cans tomato sauce
1½ cups water
2 bay leaves
  salt
  pepper

Using a long knife, make a wide slit lengthwise through the center of the roast. Stuff the chorizos into this opening, one after another, along the length of the meat.

Heat lard or olive oil in a large Dutch oven or roasting pan. Add meat and brown on all sides. When meat is half browned, add garlic, onions and pepper. Continue cooking until the onions are golden.

Add tomato sauce, water, bay leaves and salt and pepper to taste. Cover pot and place in 350° oven. Roast until meat is tender (about 2 hours).

PUDÍN DIPLOMÁTICO (SERVES 8)

  1 quart milk
  1 lemon rind, grated
  1 cinnamon stick
  6 eggs
  2 teaspoons vanilla extract
1¾ cups sugar
  ½ jigger crème de cacao
  1 cup fruit cocktail
  4 slices white bread, with crusts removed

Bring milk to boil with lemon rind and cinnamon stick. Pour milk through strainer, to remove flavorings and the skin formed by boiling.

Beat eggs very well. Add milk, vanilla, ¾ cup sugar and crème de cacao. Beat well.

Melt 1 cup sugar over high heat. Heat until sugar syrup turns brown and begins to bubble. Spread this caramel syrup in a 9×9-inch baking pan, coating it well. Pour in egg-and-milk mixture. Stir in fruit cocktail. Top with bread slices and bake at 450° for 40 minutes. Let cool, chill and serve.

POT AU FEU

123 WEST 49TH STREET
NEW YORK CITY
756-4840

One of the most appealing things about Pot au Feu is that it has a clearly defined purpose: it exists to serve soups and stews to a large number of people in an efficient and graceful manner. The owners and designers have given careful attention to all the details of the operation, from the molded plastic trays to the paintings on the walls, from the texture of the breads to the placement of the tables. The result is both interesting and pleasant. The restaurant emerges as an attractive haven where one may enjoy a modestly priced, nourishing and unusual meal.

Located on the ground floor of the Exxon Building at Rockefeller Center, Pot au Feu occupies a huge space which has been cleverly broken up into several distinct dining areas. Noteworthy features include a waterfall, an outdoor area for fair-weather dining, a small cocktail lounge open evenings from 4:30 to 9:00 P.M. and an attractive U-shaped counter where one may choose from the day's offerings. While making the most of contemporary design and production techniques, the restaurant retains a distinctly personal ambiance, thanks largely to the attentions of co-owners Billie Royce and Stefani Sheresky.

The recipes we received have all been developed by Pot au Feu's executive chef, Alfred Wiedmer. The Vienna Chicken Stew is particularly good and easy. Pot au Feu is a good version of an old favorite, and the lentil soup is a rich and flavorful one. Apple Cobbler, a slightly complicated dessert, is outstanding.

LENTIL SOUP WITH BAUERNWURST (SERVES 8)

1 clove garlic
1 tablespoon salt
4 tablespoons lard or bacon fat
1 large onion, diced
1 cup lentils
2 cups diced carrots
1 ham bone
1 bay leaf
2 cloves
½ teaspoon pepper
3 quarts beef stock or water
2 cups diced potatoes
1 pound bauernwurst or kielbasy, sliced thin
2 tablespoons vinegar (optional)

Mash garlic with salt. Melt lard or bacon in heavy kettle. Add onions and garlic. Sauté until onions are translucent. Add lentils, carrots, ham bone, bay leaf, cloves, pepper and water. Cover and simmer for 30 minutes.

Add potatoes and adjust seasoning with salt and pepper if necessary. Remove ham bone and add bauernwurst or kielbasy. Simmer until potatoes are tender (about 15 minutes). Stir in vinegar, if desired, just before serving.

BEEF BARLEY SOUP WITH MUSHROOMS (SERVES 8)

2 tablespoons butter
½ cup chopped onions
1 pound beef in ½-inch cubes
2 tablespoons flour
3 quarts water
1 pound beef bones
1 cup pearl barley (large)
1 large carrot, diced
1 stalk celery, diced
1 teaspoon white pepper
1 bay leaf
2 cloves
1 tablespoon salt
1 pound fresh mushrooms, sliced
1 cup heavy cream
2 tablespoons chopped parsley

Heat butter in large kettle. Sauté onions and beef until beef is browned. Stir in flour and brown a few minutes. Add water, beef bones, barley, carrot, celery and all seasonings. Bring to boil and simmer, covered, for 1 hour, until beef is tender and barley is cooked.

Remove beef bones. Add mushrooms and simmer a few minutes. Remove 1 cup of broth from soup and blend with cream. Return this to the soup and stir in well. Remove from heat. Sprinkle with parsley and serve.

POT AU FEU (SERVES 8)

2 pounds beef (chuck or brisket)
2 frying chickens (1½ pounds each, left whole)
2 stalks celery
1 onion
1 carrot
2 bay leaves
3 cloves
1 clove garlic
  dash of nutmeg
1 teaspoon salt
¼ teaspoon peppercorns

2 stalks celery, diced
2 carrots, diced
3 turnips, diced
12 pearl onions
½ green cabbage, diced
2 stalks leek, diced
2 whole scallions, chopped
6 ounces medium noodles

Place beef and chicken in large kettle with celery, onion, carrot and seasonings. Cover with about 6 quarts of water. Bring to boil and simmer, uncovered. After 20 minutes (or when tender), remove chickens. Continue cooking beef for two hours, or until done. Remove beef. Strain broth and reserve.

Skin and bone chicken and cube. Cube beef. Boil remaining vegetables in salted water for about 15 minutes, just until tender. Boil noodles in salted water for 10 minutes.

Strain noodles and add to broth. Add vegetables, chicken and beef. Adjust seasoning with salt and freshly ground pepper. Mix thoroughly and heat before serving. Sprinkle with scallions.

VIENNA CHICKEN STEW (SERVES 6)

2 tablespoons butter
2 tablespoons vegetable oil
2 frying chickens (2½ pounds each), cut into chunks
  salt
  pepper
3 medium onions, chopped
1 clove garlic, minced
2½ tablespoons flour
2 tablespoons Hungarian paprika
1 cup chicken broth
2 cups sour cream

Heat butter and oil in large casserole. Add chicken and sauté till golden brown. Season with salt and pepper. Add onions and garlic and sauté till onions are translucent. Add flour and paprika and stir in well. Add chicken broth and sour cream. Mix well, cover and simmer for 20 minutes until chicken is tender and sauce is thickened and smooth. Serve with potato pancakes or noodles.

APPLE COBBLER (16 SERVINGS)

SWEET DOUGH

½ pound butter
1 cup sugar
3 eggs
1 pound flour

Blend butter and sugar. Beat in eggs. Add flour and mix well. Roll out until ⅛ to ¼ inch thick and bake in 350° oven until light brown (about 30 minutes).

APPLE FILLING

  2 cups water
  1 cup sugar
½ teaspoon cinnamon
  2 tablespoons cornstarch dissolved in ¼ cup water
  2 pounds apples, peeled and sliced

Place water, sugar and cinnamon in saucepan. Bring to boil, add cornstarch and mix in well. Add apples and stir in well. Remove from heat.

STREUSEL DOUGH

  1 pound flour
  1 cup sugar
½ pound almond paste
½ teaspoon cinnamon

Mix all ingredients, then crumble into a baking pan. Bake at 350° until light brown (about 30 minutes).

VANILLA CREAM

1 pint heavy cream
3 ounces vanilla powder or 1 tablespoon vanilla extract

Beat cream with vanilla until you get a thick sauce.

To serve, break pieces of Sweet Dough into dessert bowl. Cover with Apple Filling. Add Streusel Dough and top with Vanilla Cream.

LA POTAGERIE

554 FIFTH AVENUE
NEW YORK CITY
586-7790

We learn from La Potagerie's press releases that soup in the Western world originated with the medieval custom of "sopping." This was a dining habit developed at a time when fingers were the primary utensils. To fully enjoy the liquid part of stews, nobles and peasants alike are said to have sponged up their broth with bread. Eventually, the "sop"—or "soupe" (in French)— was promoted to a liquid meal in itself, known as potage. Hence, "La Potagerie," a dining establishment devoted exclusively to soup and a few accompaniments.

In the few years since its opening, La Potagerie has become a Fifth Avenue classic, a stylish haven where you can relax with a large bowl of soup and enjoy the sparkling design of the interior. Executive chef Jacques Pepin, formerly chef to Charles de Gaulle and once director of research and food development for Howard Johnson's, brings a unique combination of classic French cooking skill and mass-production techniques to the operation. M. Pepin believes that Americans are belatedly learning to appreciate the subtleties of fine food, and he was happy to share his recipes with us to further the cause of good taste on this side of the Atlantic.

SPLIT PEA SOUP (SERVES 8 TO 10)

¾ pound bacon, chopped coarsely
1½ pounds split peas
2 pounds potatoes, peeled and diced
1 cup diced celery
1 cup diced onions
2 10¾-ounce cans each of condensed or concentrated beef broth and chicken broth
2 leeks, sliced
1 tablespoon salt
½ teaspoon freshly ground black pepper
½ teaspoon thyme leaves
2 tablespoons grated horseradish

Place half of bacon in a baking tray and brown in oven.

Place peas, potatoes, onions, celery, broth, leeks, salt, pepper, thyme and remaining bacon in a kettle. Add enough water to reach approximately 1½ inches above the ingredients. Bring to a boil, and simmer for 2½ hours. Add water if the liquid evaporates too quickly. Mix every 10 minutes with a whisk to avoid scorching.

When the soup is cooked, whip with the whisk, or use an electric beater to break down the potatoes and peas into smooth soup. Add the browned bacon and cook another 10 minutes. Add the horseradish.

To serve, garnish each bowl with 1 tablespoon each of chopped celery and grated Swiss cheese. Add salt and pepper to taste.

GOULASH DE VEAU HONGROISE (SERVES 8 TO 10)

1 pound lean veal, cut into 1-inch cubes
1 pound onions, thinly sliced
3 tablespoons sharp Hungarian paprika
1 teaspoon caraway seed
1½ tablespoons salt
½ teaspoon ground white pepper
¾ cup tomato paste
2 8-ounce cans stewed tomatoes
4 10-ounce cans chicken broth

1½ sticks sweet butter
1½ cups flour
¾ cup spaetzle

3 cloves garlic, chopped fine
2 cups half-and-half
1 cup heavy sweet cream
2 cups sour cream

Place veal in a pan, cover with water and bring to a boil. Immediately pour veal into a strainer and rinse. Place in a large kettle. Add onions, paprika, caraway seed, salt, pepper, tomato paste, stewed tomatoes and broth. Add enough water to barely cover meat. Bring to a boil and simmer gently for 1½ hours.

Melt butter, add flour and mix together. After the soup has simmered for 1½ hours, remove the meat. Add spaetzle and boil for 5 minutes. Then add flour-and-butter mixture, stirring to avoid lumps.

Return meat to pot and simmer another 15 minutes. Add garlic, half-and-half, and sweet and sour cream. Stir, bring to a boil and serve.

WALL STREET CHOWDER (SERVES 6 TO 8)

   3 slices bacon, coarsely chopped
  ¼ cup diced onion
  ¼ cup diced carrots
   2 tablespoons diced celery
   1 tablespoon diced white turnips
   2 tablespoons diced eggplant
   2 tablespoons diced cabbage
   2 tablespoons diced zucchini
   2 tablespoons diced green pepper
   1 tablespoon diced broccoli rape or fennel bulb
   1 tablespoon tomato paste
  ¼ cup diced whole tomato
     dash each of oregano, bay leaf, thyme, salt, pepper
  ½ pound chopped clams
   5 cups beef or chicken broth

Melt bacon in Dutch kettle. Add onions and sauté 4 to 5 minutes. Add all the other ingredients and simmer, covered, 1½ hours. If too much liquid evaporates, add water to maintain quantity of soup.

LENTIL SOUP (SERVES 6 TO 8)

   3 slices bacon, coarsely chopped
   1 leek, diced
   1 small onion, diced
   1 cup lentils (soaked for 2 hours)

1 carrot, diced
1 clove garlic, crushed and chopped
2 potatoes, diced
  salt, pepper
1½ quarts chicken or beef stock

Melt bacon and sauté leek and onion for a few minutes. Add remaining ingredients and simmer slowly for 2 hours. Add water if necessary. Before serving, break the big pieces by whipping the soup by hand or with an electric beater. Serve with diced ham.

VEGETABLE SOUP

1 onion, sliced thin
2 leeks, sliced thin
2 tablespoons sweet butter
½ cup thinly sliced cabbage
¾ cup sliced celery
½ cup thinly sliced carrots
⅓ cup thinly sliced white turnips
1½ quarts chicken stock
2 cups thinly sliced potatoes
  salt and pepper to taste
2 tablespoons chopped parsley

Sauté onions and leeks in the butter for a few minutes. Add cabbage, celery, carrots and turnips, and sauté a few more minutes. Add stock and bring to a boil. Simmer for 30 minutes. Add the potatoes, salt and pepper, and simmer another 30 minutes. Top with chopped parsley.

CREAM OF CHICKEN SOUP (SERVES 6 TO 8)

½ cup sweet butter
½ cup flour
1½ quarts Chicken Stock (see below)
  salt and pepper to taste
¾ cup heavy cream
1 carrot, cut in thin strips
1 leek, cut in thin strips
  chicken meat (from stock, below), cut in strips
5 mushrooms, cut in strips

Melt butter, mix in flour and cook gently for 3 or 4 minutes. Add all but ½ cup of the strained stock and whisk carefully. Bring to a boil and simmer 5 to 10 minutes. Add salt and pepper if needed. Add the cream and bring to a boil again.

Cook carrot and leek in ½ cup stock for 5 to 10 minutes. Add this to the soup, along with the chicken meat and mushrooms. Keep covered in a double boiler.

CHICKEN STOCK

1 small hen (about 1½ pounds)
1 small onion
  thyme
  bay leaf
  whole pepper
  salt
  sprigs of parsley
2 quarts water

Simmer for 1½ hours. Strain, reserving chicken. Should yield 1½ quarts of broth.

LE HOCHEPOT (SERVES 6 TO 8)

¼ cup diced carrots
½ cup diced onions
½ cup diced celery
¼ cup diced white turnips
¼ cup diced leek
2 tablespoons sweet butter
1½ quarts Lamb Stock (see below)
½ cup diced lamb
⅓ cup barley
  salt
  pepper
  Worcestershire sauce
  freshly chopped parsley

Sauté vegetables in butter for a few minutes. Add the stock, lamb and barley. Simmer for 1¼ hours. Season with salt, pepper and Worcestershire sauce, and sprinkle with chopped parsley.

LAMB STOCK

1 pound lamb bones
4 or 5 juniper berries
2 quarts water
  dash each of thyme, salt, pepper

Cook for 1½ hours, adding water to maintain quantity. Should yield 1½ quarts.

POT AU MONACO (SERVES 6 TO 8)

½ cup diced onions
2 tablespoons fresh fennel
2 tablespoons olive oil
¼ cup diced eggplant
¼ cup diced zucchini
¼ cup diced cabbage
2 cloves garlic, crushed
2 tablespoons tomato paste
¼ cup diced tomatoes
   salt
   pepper
   thyme
   basil
1½ quarts water
1 cup dry white wine
1 pound fish bones (tied up in cheesecloth)
2 tablespoons orzo macaroni
1 teaspoon saffron pistils

Sauté onions and fennel in oil for 4 to 5 minutes. Add eggplant, zucchini, cabbage, garlic, tomato paste and fresh tomato, salt, pepper, thyme, basil, water and wine. Cook for 10 minutes. Add the fish bones and cook for 30 minutes. Remove the fish bones. Add the orzo and saffron. Cook for 15 minutes. Serve with cubes of fish, mussels and toasted French bread rubbed with garlic.

BORGHESE GARDEN VEGETABLE SOUP
(SERVES 6 TO 8)

1 piece short ribs of beef
2 quarts water
1 pig knuckle
1 clove
  dash each of salt and pepper
  thyme
1 tomato, diced
½ carrot, diced
¼ cup diced celery
¼ cup diced cabbage
¼ cup diced turnips
¼ cup diced string beans
¼ cup diced zucchini
¼ cup diced onion
¼ cup diced leek
3 tablespoons tomato paste

1 clove garlic
1 tablespoon parsley
1 tablespoon chervil
1 tablespoon basil
3 tablespoons back fat
½ cup broken spaghetti
  Parmesan cheese

Cook first group of ingredients slowly for 1½ hours. Make a purée from garlic, parsley, chervil, basil and back fat. Add to the soup, with spaghetti. Cook for 20 minutes and garnish with Parmesan.

THE PUGLIA RESTAURANT

189 HESTER STREET
NEW YORK CITY
226-8912

Every Friday and Saturday night there's a party at Puglia's. Waiters dancing between tables; people talking in loud, excited voices; a heavy Italian woman singing Italian, Jewish and American songs to the accompaniment of guitar, accordion and clapping; a family celebrating a birthday or wedding anniversary in the back; everyone cheerfully, unabashedly drunk on the house red wine, which flows freely and is available for $2.50 a bottle—it's a frenzied, heady, non-American atmosphere, and it's always best to go with more than two people. Neighbors at the long tables invariably talk with each other, share bread and wine, and part friends.

The food, rushed out of the kitchen by the nimble-footed waiters, is tasty and fairly priced. During the day the restaurant is frequented by neighborhood old-timers, who linger lovingly over the southern Italian specialties, which, though not unsatisfying, are a far cry from haute cuisine. Puglia is not a place for those with delicate eating habits or sensibilities, but for those who can appreciate the most highly spiced, greasiest garlic bread in New York, this is the place.

BROCCOLI RAPE (SERVES 4)

2 pounds broccoli rape
½ head fresh garlic, coarsely minced
1 cup olive oil

Wash rape and trim about 1 inch off the bottom of each stalk. Do not cut into pieces; try to use a pot that is roomy enough for the full plant.

In large pot, heat garlic in olive oil until oil starts to bubble lightly. Do *not* allow the garlic to brown.

Add the rape to the oil and garlic. Cover, and steam over low heat for about 20 minutes. Shake the pot occasionally to distribute the oil and keep the rape from sticking to the bottom. The broccoli should be deep green and tender, soft but not limp.

There's a special gleam in the eye of Joe Garofalo, owner of Puglia, when he talks about broccoli rape (pronounced "broccoli raab"). A staple in northern Italy, it's one of those foods always forced on the children, and always violently hated by them. But thanks to his chef, Semeia Gallisto, Joe has learned to love the bitter green, claiming he can eat it for breakfast, lunch and dinner. As our neighborhood Italian grocer says, "When you grow older, you learn to appreciate the bitter foods."

The vegetable comes to you complete with stalks, leaves and lovely flowers; if you can't find it in your supermarket, try the nearest Italian greengrocer, and watch the delight as he brings out your order. The final result in this recipe tastes something like broccoli—a little like spinach—reminiscent of dandelion greens. But mostly it's delicious, and great served with plain spaghetti.

PASTA E FAGIOLE (SERVES 4 TO 6)

3   stalks celery
2   large tomatoes, peeled
1   cup white kidney beans
½   head garlic (about 5 cloves, whole)
3   or 4 bay leaves
1   tablespoon salt
1   teaspoon pepper
2   to 3 tablespoons olive oil
8   cups water

1   cup tubettini (and/or any other small pasta)

The night before you plan to serve, cut up the celery and tomatoes to about the size of the dried beans. Place beans, vegetables, whole peeled garlic cloves, bay leaves, salt, pepper and olive oil in large pot and cover with the water. Stir it up and let it sit, uncovered, at least 12 hours.

Bring water and its flavorings to a boil, cover and simmer gently for 2 hours, stirring occasionally.

Boil pasta for about half the time necessary to cook thoroughly. Drain, add to the bean mixture and simmer until pasta is *al dente*. Serve.

LUPINIS

Although these are not served at Puglia's, Joe Garofalo offered the recipe as a characteristic Italian snack.

1 pound lupini beans

Place lupinis in pot and add water to twice the depth of the beans. Cover and simmer until beans are tender.

Drain beans and place in large bowl. Cover with water. Soak for 7 days, changing water daily. At end of week, drain beans, season with salt and serve.

CIPPOLINI SALAD (SERVES 4 TO 6)

1 pound cippolini
  olive oil
  minced garlic
  chopped parsley
  salt
  pepper

Wash cippolini. Boil in water until tender (about 20 minutes). Drain and let cool. Peel cippolini and remove hard portion from top and bottom. Chill. Serve with olive oil, garlic, parsley, salt and pepper to taste.

FRIED CIPPOLINI (SERVES 4 TO 6)

1 pound cippolini
  flour
2 eggs, beaten
  oil

Boil cippolini and peel as in recipe for Cippolini Salad. Mash each lightly with a fork. Dredge in flour, then dip in beaten egg. Deep-fry until golden brown. Drain and serve.

RALPH'S

347 FIRST AVENUE
NEW YORK CITY
GR 7-7180

Ralph's is a quiet, formica-tabled Italian restaurant/pizzeria run by Sicilian-born Ralph Ferrante and his charming wife, Lucy. For 20 years now, Ralph has been doing all the cooking, with Lucy serving as waitress and hostess; most recently she has been accompanied by their friendly poodle, Ricky. The restaurant, which has a comfortable, homey atmosphere, serves delicately prepared Italian food. Ralph, formerly a foreman for LaRosa, keeps a watchful eye on his pasta and serves it consistently al dente. The secret of Ralph's cooking seems to be the happy combination of garlic, parsley, high-quality olive oil and imported Italian canned tomatoes. The following recipes are both simple and delicious.

SHRIMPS FRA DIAVOLO (SERVES 2)

10 jumbo shrimp, cleaned
 5 tablespoons chopped parsley
 2 teaspoons minced garlic
 2 tablespoons olive oil
 2 16-ounce cans Italian tomatoes
 1 teaspoon salt
¼ teaspoon pepper
 4 littleneck clams

Sauté shrimp, parsley and garlic in olive oil until garlic and shrimp are lightly browned. Add tomatoes, salt, pepper and clams. Stir well, cover and simmer gently for 20 minutes. Serve with spaghetti or macaroni.

TOMATO SAUCE (TO SERVE OVER SPAGHETTI AND FOR USE IN THE VEAL PARMIGIANA BELOW)

1 20-ounce can Italian tomatoes (imported!)
3 cloves garlic, minced
1 medium onion, chopped
½ cup chopped parsley
  dash of oregano
  salt and pepper to taste

Combine all ingredients and simmer, covered, for 2 to 3 hours.

VEAL CUTLET PARMIGIANA (SERVES 4 TO 6)

1 cup bread crumbs
2 cloves garlic, minced
3 tablespoons chopped parsley
1 cup grated Parmesan cheese
1 pound veal cutlets
  flour
3 eggs, beaten
  olive oil
1 to 2 cups Tomato Sauce
½ pound mozzarella cheese, cut into thin strips

Combine bread crumbs, garlic, parsley and 2 tablespoons grated Parmesan. Dip veal in flour, then in beaten eggs, and coat with bread-crumb mixture.

Pour olive oil into baking dish so that it is about 1 inch deep. Heat in 350° oven for about 10 minutes. Now slip breaded cutlets into the hot oil and bake for 8 minutes.

Remove veal from oil and pour off oil. Lay veal in baking dish, covering each slice with some mozzarella, Parmesan and Tomato Sauce. Pour remaining Tomato Sauce over veal, and top generously with mozzarella and Parmesan. Bake 10 to 15 minutes, until cheese is thoroughly melted.

This is an unusual recipe for veal Parmesan, since it does not require that the breaded veal be deep-fried. Instead it is gently heated in the olive oil and emerges so tender you can cut it with a fork.

CLAM SAUCE (SERVES 2)

    2 teaspoons chopped parsley
    2 teaspoons minced garlic
    4 tablespoons olive oil
   16 fresh clams, cleaned and chopped
      juice from clams

Brown parsley and garlic in olive oil. Add clams and juice, and simmer gently 5 to 10 minutes. Serve over spaghetti.

EL RANCHO ARGENTINO

28 WEST 31ST STREET
NEW YORK CITY
565-9620

It would be difficult to prepare the most popular offerings of the Rancho Argentino at home—for these are the famous Argentinian steaks, prepared and cut in the Argentine manner, then charcoal-broiled on a very hot grill. The butchering technique is held in considerable secrecy by owner/chef Buffanti, and seems to be inaccessible to Americans. Then there's the charcoal broiling—essential for the true gaucho flavor, but not very feasible in most kitchens.

Fortunately, Empanadas and Matambre, two unique Argentinian specialties, are easily reproduced in the home kitchen. Though time-consuming, the Empanadas are well worth making. They may be prepared in large quantities and frozen for future use. Rancho Argentino's version of this classic "gaucho pie" is excellent—nothing like the dry, smelly version sold at corner stands throughout the city—and we urge you to get out your rolling pin and prepare a batch for your next party.

EMPANADAS (ABOUT 3 DOZEN 6-INCH PIES)

1½ pounds ground beef
  1 pound onions, chopped fine
  2 tablespoons lard
  2 green peppers, chopped

 6 hard-boiled eggs, chopped
20 to 30 stuffed olives, chopped
¾ cup raisins
 1 teaspoon salt
 1 tablespoon ground or whole cumin seed

 3 pounds white flour
 1 tablespoon salt
 1 cup lard
 3 cups water
 1 pound lard

Sauté beef and onions in 2 tablespoons lard until meat is browned but not dry. Add peppers, eggs, olives, raisins, salt and cumin. Simmer about 10 minutes, stirring well. Taste and correct seasoning. You may add some liquid from the olives. Let cool.

Combine flour and salt. Cut in 1 cup lard and add water slowly, mixing well. Turn onto board and knead until dough is smooth and does not stick to hands or board. Roll out as thin as possible (less than ⅛ inch) and cut into circles about 6 inches in diameter (use a coffee-can cover or other circular die).

Place about 1 tablespoon of meat mixture in center of each circle. Fold over and pinch edges together, sealing with water. Then, beginning at one corner, fold the edge back in small, overlapping sections, to create fluting.

In large pot, heat 1 pound lard to 350°. Slip empanadas into fat; they will drop immediately to the bottom and rise when ready (about 5 minutes). Drain on paper towels and serve immediately.

MATAMBRE (SERVES 6 TO 8)

1 piece top of the rib (beef)—about 2 pounds, 8×12×½ inches
1½ carrots, sliced lengthwise as thin as possible
1 onion, chopped
4 cloves garlic, minced
¾ cup parsley, chopped
1 teaspoon crushed red pepper
2 teaspoons salt
2 teaspoons oregano
4 or 5 hard-boiled eggs

Remove most of the fat from the meat. Lay strips of carrot lengthwise across the meat. Sprinkle with onions, garlic, parsley, red pepper, salt and oregano. Along the length of the meat lay the hard-boiled eggs, end to end. Now roll the meat around the eggs as tightly as possible. Sew the roll together with string, sealing both ends and looping the string around the meat to keep it firmly rolled. Place in large pot and cover with water. Cover. Bring to boil, reduce heat and simmer until meat is tender (about 1½ hours). Drain meat and chill. Serve cold, cut into slices.

RED TULIP HUNGARIAN RESTAURANT

250 EAST 83RD STREET
NEW YORK CITY
734-9527

Marianne Kovacs left her native Hungarian village in 1957, coming alone to the United States to attend college and to find a better life. Though she has succeeded in finding that life, she continues to treasure her vivid childhood memories above all. Those memories have been given a permanent home in the Red Tulip, the delightful restaurant Mrs. Kovacs opened recently with her husband, Kazmer.

The Kovacses by their own efforts have transformed a burned and useless storefront on East 83rd Street into a charming reproduction of a traditional Hungarian dining room. Mr. Kovacs carved and built the handsome wood chairs and tables himself, in addition to installing walls, floors, plumbing and wiring.

The cooking in the restaurant is done by Mrs. Kovacs. Her husband serves as the waiter. An imaginative and enthusiastic chef, Mrs. Kovacs works hard to make her creations as tasty and authentic as possible, taking great pleasure in preparing the dishes she has loved since childhood. We learned from her that the "proper" (Hungarian) way to chop vegetables is to not use a cutting board. You hold the onion (or tomato, or pepper, or garlic) in one hand, turning it while you make the appropriate incisions with a knife held in the other. The technique requires steady hands and careful control of the knife; once mastered, though, it can be performed with a minimum of effort and a maximum of ease. Mrs. Kovacs and her mother (who was in New York helping out when we visited the restaurant's kitchen) were beautiful to watch as they quietly sliced their vegetables with small, graceful movements whose traditions reached far back into time.

For all its evocations of the past, though, the Red Tulip is a thoroughly contemporary restaurant, functioning quite nicely in the present. The Kovacses are happily at home in the life of New York, and as fluent in the new culture as in the old. Such a synthesis is rare and captivating. It is the basis of the Red Tulip's success.

VEAL CUTLETS (SERVES 2)

½ cup water
½ cup vegetable oil
1 heaping tablespoon whole black peppercorns
½ to ¾ pound veal cutlets, pounded
   salt
5 cloves garlic, minced
1½ green peppers, sliced

Place water, oil and peppercorns in skillet. Add veal and sprinkle with salt. Cover with garlic and peppers. Cover pan and bring to boil over high heat. Lower flame and simmer one to 1½ hours, until most of the liquid is evaporated and the veal is lightly browned. While it is cooking, shake pan occasionally. Serve as is, or with the following sauce:

Strain pan juices into a blender, mashing the peppers to extract all their liquid. Skim off fat. For each cup of juice, heat 1 tablespoon fat in skillet. Add 1 tablespoon flour and brown lightly. Add 1 tablespoon tomato purée and blend in well.

Add to juices in the blender. Add ¼ cup Hungarian white wine (Leanyka) and blend well. Serve.

VEAL SHANK (SERVES 1 OR 2)

1 veal shank
  salt
  ground black pepper
  garlic powder
  ground ginger
  ground allspice
  ground marjoram and/or marjoram leaves
  ground nutmeg
  ground cloves
  thyme
1 clove garlic, crushed
4 tablespoons double-smoked bacon fat (or butter or oil; double-smoked bacon fat is a delicacy available in Hungarian butcher shops)
1 cup water

Wash shank well. Sprinkle generously with each of the dry seasonings, being especially liberal with the thyme. Rub the garlic clove into the meat, working in all the other seasonings as you do this. You may also rub the veal with some prepared chicken-soup base.

Place the meat on a rack in a pressure cooker. Add 1 tablespoon fat and water. Cover and steam for 20 minutes.

When veal is done, remove from pressure cooker and sear in 3 tablespoons hot bacon fat, turning so that meat is reddish brown on all sides. Cover with vegetables, prepared as follows:

2 tablespoons double-smoked bacon fat
1 large onion, sliced
2 or 3 green peppers, sliced
2 fresh tomatoes, peeled and quartered

marjoram
garlic powder
black pepper
salt
sugar
2 cups sliced mushrooms
1 tablespoon vegetable oil

Melt fat and gently sauté onions until golden. Add green peppers and continue to sauté another 5 to 10 minutes. Add tomatoes. Sprinkle with marjoram, garlic powder, pepper and salt.
Add ½ to 1 teaspoon sugar to taste. Mix well, cover and simmer
about 5 minutes.

Meanwhile, sauté mushrooms in oil just until they are tender.
Mix in with other vegetables and serve immediately over the veal.

CHICKEN LIVERS RED TULIP (SERVES 2)

chicken fat
1 large onion, sliced
2 or 3 green peppers, sliced
salt
1 cup sliced mushrooms
10 chicken livers
garlic powder
black pepper

Melt 1 or 2 tablespoons chicken fat in a skillet. Sauté onions
until golden brown. Add green peppers and sprinkle with salt.
Sauté for 5 to 10 minutes, until peppers are thoroughly cooked.

In a separate skillet, sauté mushrooms in 1 tablespoon chicken
fat just until tender. Stir into pepper-and-onion mixture.

In a small saucepan, melt chicken fat, using enough to have
about 1 inch of liquid fat. Heat well, then add livers over very

high heat. Cover and fry for 2 minutes. Turn off heat and wait a minute or two. Turn livers over, cover again and turn on heat. Fry again for 2 minutes, then allow to sit a few minutes longer. Drain livers and add to the vegetable mixture. Sprinkle with garlic powder, salt and black pepper. Over medium heat, cook all together for a few minutes, stirring constantly and shaking pan. Serve.

POTATO DUMPLINGS (MAKES ABOUT 15 1-INCH DUMPLINGS)

3 medium potatoes
1 teaspoon salt
1 or 2 eggs
  about ¾ cup flour
  vegetable oil

Peel potatoes, slice and boil in salted water until tender.

Drain and mash potatoes. Add egg(s) and mix in well. Now add flour, using only enough to absorb the liquid and to create a firm dough-like paste. Using floured hands, roll this dough into balls about 1 inch in diameter. Roll balls in flour.

Heat oil in saucepan (it should be about 1½ inches deep). Add dumplings and fry over medium high heat until deep brown in color. Turn dumplings regularly while they are frying. Drain and serve immediately.

SAKURA CHAYA

198 COLUMBUS AVENUE
NEW YORK CITY
874-8536

Sakura Chaya is an unpretentious, pleasant restaurant, colorfully adorned with Japanese prints, artificial autumn leaves and live green plants. The food is carefully prepared and attractively served, and though the tables are rather closely packed, privacy is possible. There is a small sushi bar, where one may sample numerous varieties of raw fish served with cold, vinegared rice.

Aki, Sakura Chaya's cheerful and capable owner, is a man who believes strongly in the virtues of sushi. "God never told us to cook fish," he exclaimed, when asked how this uniquely Japanese tradition developed. As popular in Japan as sandwiches are in the United States, sushi is beginning to gain acceptance here, and Aki loves to acquaint his customers with this unique health and taste treat. He insisted, however, that the techniques for preparing sushi can only be learned from a master, and require long years of study. Thus, he was unable to provide us with any sushi recipes. Instead, he offered the following instructions for Sakura Chaya's delicate and delicious Bean Sprout Salad, the unusual Negi Maki and the standard but good Sukiyaki. Sakura Chaya's sauces are particularly interesting, and we recommend them for use in other Japanese recipes.

SUKIYAKI (SERVES 2)

1⅓ pounds shell steak
½ cup sliced mushrooms
½ cup diced bean curd
½ cup sliced bamboo shoots
½ cup sliced onion
½ cup Chinese cabbage, cut into 1-inch squares
4 scallions, cut into thin strips
½ cup boiled glass noodles

Remove all fat from beef and reserve. Slice beef as thin as possible.

In a large skillet, heat the fat. Add Sukiyaki Sauce (see below). Add beef and cook over high flame for 2 minutes. Add vegetables and noodles, and simmer for 10 minutes.

SUKIYAKI SAUCE

2 cups water
1 piece kombu (about 2×5 inches)
handful dried bonito flakes
1½ cups soy sauce
1 cup sugar
¼ cup sake

In a saucepan, bring water, kombu and bonito flakes to a boil. Remove from heat and strain. Let broth cool.

Add soy sauce, sugar and sake. Mix well.

NEGI MAKI (SERVES 2)

1 pound beef, sliced as thin as possible
2 bunches scallions, washed

Lay half of beef on table, placing several slices end to end to create a length equal to the scallion length. Do the same with the second portion. Place one bunch scallions on each layer of beef. Roll beef tightly around the scallions and secure with bamboo sticks or toothpicks. Broil until beef is well done (about 5 to 10 minutes). Remove sticks and cut rolls into ½-inch segments. Stand these up on a plate, cover with Tare Sauce and heat briefly before serving.

TARE SAUCE

2 cups soy sauce
2 cups dry sherry
2 cloves garlic, minced
1 teaspoon minced ginger
1 stalk celery, sliced thin
1 carrot, sliced thin
1 onion, sliced thin
2 cups sugar
1 teaspoon salt

Combine all ingredients and bring to a boil. Simmer, uncovered, for 30 minutes, or until all the alcohol has evaporated. Let cool to room temperature. (Do not refrigerate.)

BEAN SPROUT SALAD (SERVES 2)

1 cup bean sprouts
3 tablespoons rice vinegar
⅛ teaspoon sesame oil
¼ teaspoon soy sauce
⅛ teaspoon salt
⅛ teaspoon sugar
1 tablespoon sesame seeds

Steam sprouts over boiling water for 2 or 3 minutes. Cool on ice cubes, and drain off all water.

Combine remaining ingredients for dressing. Toss with bean sprouts and serve.

SCHAEFER'S

1202 LEXINGTON AVENUE
NEW YORK CITY
734-9887

*The offerings at Schaefer's are all solidly German, straightfor-
ward and hearty. The restaurant is unpretentious and quiet, with
a long counter and a few small tables. It has recently changed
hands. Käthe Heerdegen, the longtime owner, has left. Werner
Pfarrer is now in charge. Mrs. Heerdegen gave us the following
recipes before she retired. (Mr. Pfarrer says he is using the same
methods.)*

*The Red Cabbage below is a common German side dish, and it
provides a refreshing change from the usual green vegetables
served in America. It is simple, economical and quite tasty. Mrs.
Heerdegen had warned us not to overcook—the vegetables should
be tender, not limp.*

SAUERBRATEN (SERVES 4 TO 6)

1 cup water
2 cups white vinegar
2 onions, sliced
1 tablespoon pickling (mixed) spice
2 tablespoons salt
2 tablespoons sugar
2 pounds bottom round roast

Combine water, vinegar, onions and seasonings. Bring to a
boil and let cool.

Pour marinade over meat and refrigerate, uncovered, for one week.

Remove meat from marinade, rinse well and pat dry. Brown on all sides in hot fat. Bake in 350° oven for 1 to 1½ hours.

Prepare a gravy from the drippings, thickening with 1 part flour to 2 parts cornstarch. Serve.

GERMAN RED CABBAGE (SERVES 4)

3 tablespoons lard or vegetable shortening
1 medium red cabbage, shredded
¼ cup white vinegar, heated
1 bay leaf
2 onions, sliced
1 large McIntosh apple cored and cut into large cubes
1 cup beef stock (bouillon or water may be used instead)
2 tablespoons sauerkraut
1 to 2 teaspoons cornstarch

Melt shortening in large saucepan. Add cabbage, cover, and stew gently for about 5 minutes, shaking pot to prevent scorching. Add hot vinegar, bay leaf and onions, and stew another 10 minutes. Now add apple and stock, mix well and simmer very gently 40 to 45 minutes.

Add rinsed sauerkraut and cook 5 minutes longer. Dissolve cornstarch in cold water and add to the cabbage mixture, simmering just until the cabbage is coated with a light, gelatinous sauce.

Lucas Gomes, knocking on his own door at Shalimar.

SHALIMAR

39 EAST 20TH STREET
NEW YORK CITY
889-1977

Lucas Gomes, the expert Indian chef and co-owner of Shalimar, happily shared these recipes with us—two specialties of the house and two Indian standards. Bhujia, or "vegetable fritters," are delicious, unmistakably Oriental treats, prepared to perfection at Shalimar. Similar in principle to the familiar tempura of Japanese and macrobiotic fame, they have a taste and texture all their own, thanks to the unique chick pea flour and the combined spices. The batter forms a thick, crunchy coating around the soft vegetables, which may be varied according to your taste and imagination. Try squash, potatoes, carrots, eggplant, bananas, onions, green peppers, chilies, spinach, cauliflower, broccoli, yams, etc.

The Boti Kebab is a curried version of shish kebab, mildly spicy and juicy. It's wonderfully easy to prepare, and if you enjoy playing with food you'll especially enjoy preparing the savory marinade, which leaves your hands smelling gently of India.

Poori, one of the varying forms of Indian bread, is quite easy to prepare and provides an excellent accompaniment for curry or stew. Firni for dessert is gentle perfection.

POORI (8 LARGE BREADS—SERVES 4)

  2 cups sifted flour, whole-wheat or white
     vegetable oil
¼ teaspoon salt

1 tablespoon milk
½ to ¾ cup lukewarm water

Combine flour, 1 teaspoon oil, salt and milk. Mix well. Slowly add lukewarm water, mixing well with your hands, until flour holds together as a soft dough.

Turn dough onto floured board and knead for at least 5 minutes, until dough has a satiny appearance. Add more flour if necessary.

Break dough into golf-ball-sized pieces, shape into balls and roll out into circles ⅛ inch thick.

Drop each circle into deep oil preheated to 360°. As soon as dough begins to puff (about 30 seconds), press poori lightly with a perforated pancake turner. Fry until poori is golden, turning once for evenness. (Total cooking time should not exceed 3 minutes.)

SAMOSA (MAKES ABOUT 1 DOZEN)

Poori dough

1½ cups chopped onion
    vegetable oil
  2 teaspoons minced ginger
  4 cloves garlic, minced
  1 teaspoon turmeric
  2 teaspoons cumin seeds
  1 teaspoon salt
  1 pound ground lamb or beef

Sauté onions in 2 tablespoons oil until translucent. Add other seasonings and cook for 1 minute. Add meat and sauté for ½ hour, until meat is very well browned and aromatic.

Prepare Poori dough as above. Roll into 3-inch circles. Place a generous tablespoon of meat mixture on each circle. Fold over into a triangle and seal dough with moistened fingers.

Deep-fry in hot oil (360° to 375°) until golden. Drain and serve.

BHUJIA (SERVES 2 TO 4)

1½ cups chick pea flour
¼ teaspoon salt
⅛ teaspoon ginger
⅜ teaspoon ground cumin
¼ teaspoon cayenne
⅛ to ¼ teaspoon chili powder
⅛ to ¼ teaspoon mustard seed
 1 clove garlic, crushed
    dash baking soda
¼ cup chopped fresh mint or coriander (optional)
 1 egg
 1 to 1½ cups cold water
 1 pound fresh vegetables
    peanut oil for deep frying

Combine flour with seasonings. Add egg and mix well. Slowly beat in water until flour is moistened and a thick, pasty batter is formed. Taste batter and add more seasonings if desired. Chill.

Wash vegetables, dry them and cut into ⅛- to ¼-inch slices. Green pepper should be cut into pieces about 1 inch square. Cauliflower should be boiled slightly and divided into flowerettes. Chili peppers may be fried whole.

Dip vegetables in batter and make sure that each piece is well coated on all sides. Drop into hot oil (350°) and let fry until batter is golden brown. Each fritter will fall to the bottom and then rise to the surface of the oil almost immediately. Turn occasionally to ensure even browning. Drain and serve.

BOTI KEBAB (SERVES 2 TO 4)

1 large onion, chopped
2 tablespoons fresh coriander, chopped
2 tablespoons cumin seed
1½ teaspoons cinnamon
1 teaspoon red pepper
2 teaspoons ginger
2 teaspoons garlic powder
½ teaspoon salt
¼ teaspoon chili powder
2 to 3 tablespoons oil
1 pound top round, cut into 1-inch cubes

1 tomato, quartered
1 onion, quartered
1 green pepper, quartered

Combine chopped onion with the 8 seasonings that follow. Mash to extract juice from the onion, then add oil and beef. Mix well and marinate in refrigerator for 24 hours.

Place pieces of beef on skewers, alternating with pieces of tomato, onion and green pepper.

Broil (if possible, on a grill) for approximately 15 minutes and serve. Watch closely during last few minutes to prevent beef from drying out.

FIRNI

4½ cups milk
 ¾ cup evaporated milk
 ⅝ cup sugar
 4 tablespoons cornstarch
 1 teaspoon rosewater
   handful of shelled, chopped pistachios

Combine 4 cups whole milk, evaporated milk and sugar. Simmer *over* boiling water for one hour.

Dissolve cornstarch in ½ cup milk. Blend very well, then stir into milk-and-sugar mixture. Simmer another 10 to 15 minutes, stirring constantly to remove all lumps.

Add rosewater and let cool. Remove skin from top of custard. Pour into mold, sprinkle with pistachios and refrigerate until firm.

SHANTI

571 THIRD AVENUE
NEW YORK CITY
867-2880

Shanti is an unpretentious, quiet Indian restaurant owned by Lucas Gomes and Vijay Bhatt, the team that runs Shalimar and Khyber. The room is a long rectangular one, completely draped (walls and ceiling) with chaddars—soft-colored Indian bedspreads. The effect is pleasant, a good backdrop for the mildly spicy, well-prepared food. We received the following recipes with instructions that one must be very precise when cooking Indian food, and we pass them on with that warning.

PORK VINDALOO (SERVES 2 TO 4)

    1 pound pork (leg), diced into ½-inch cubes
    3 tablespoons white vinegar
    ½ teaspoon salt
    5 tablespoons salad oil
    1 medium onion, chopped
    2 cinnamon sticks, broken into halves
    1 clove garlic, minced
    ½ teaspoon ground coriander
    ½ teaspoon ground cumin
    ¼ tablespoon turmeric
    ¼ tablespoon ground ginger
    ⅛ to ½ tablespoon cayenne pepper (according to taste)
    1 cup water

Wash meat well and drain. Marinate in 2 tablespoons vinegar and salt for at least 1 hour.

Heat oil in large pot. Add onions and sauté till golden. Add cinnamon sticks and garlic, and sauté for 2 to 3 minutes. Add remainder of spices and cook gently a few minutes longer. Add water and remainder of vinegar. Add pork, and cover. Bring to a boil, then reduce heat and simmer 20 to 30 minutes. Check occasionally, and add more water as needed.

VEGETABLE KOFTA (SERVES 4)

    1 pound frozen mixed vegetables
       vegetable oil
    1 onion, chopped fine
    ¼ tablespoon minced fresh ginger
    1 clove garlic, minced
    ½ tablespoon cumin seeds
    ⅛ tablespoon turmeric
    1 tablespoon salt
       pinch of cayenne
    ¼ pound chick pea flour
       Optional: 1 or 2 eggs, beaten

Cook vegetables according to instructions on package. Drain.

Heat 6 tablespoons oil in heavy pot. Sauté onion till well browned. Add seasonings and cook for 2 minutes. Stir in flour and continue to cook over low heat for 3 minutes. Add vegetables, mixing well. Cook gently for about 10 minutes until mixture is thick and sticky. Stir occasionally, adding small amounts of water if necessary.

Let vegetable mixture cool a bit. (You may prepare it a day or two in advance and refrigerate it until you are ready to serve.) Shape into balls about 2 inches in diameter. (Optional: dip balls in beaten egg. This step is omitted at the restaurant in order to keep the dish strictly vegetarian.) Deep-fry balls in hot oil until well browned. Drain.

SAUCE

    2 tablespoons vegetable oil
    1 medium onion, chopped fine
    ⅛ tablespoon turmeric
    ¼ tablespoon coriander
    ¼ tablespoon cumin
    ¼ tablespoon salt
    ⅛ to ¼ tablespoon cayenne pepper
    1 cup water

Heat oil. Add onion and sauté till golden. Add seasonings, mix well and sauté a few minutes longer, until mixture is aromatic. Add water and simmer for 5 to 10 minutes.

Place fried Kofta in Sauce and heat together for several minutes before serving.

SZECHUAN ROYAL

50 WEST 72ND STREET
NEW YORK CITY
362-2047

Among the plethora of restaurants offering "Szechuan"-style Chinese food, the Szechuan Royal is one of the best. The owner, Davy Lin, is an enterprising young businessman who has done an excellent job transforming the plain room at the Hotel Ruxton into a comfortable and quiet dining room. Mr. Lin has also opened a second Szechuan Royal, with places for 300 diners, in Patchogue, Long Island.

Once you have assembled the ingredients, each of these three dishes can be made in less than 10 minutes. Chinese cooking is fantastically fast. We watched the chef prepare both the Eggplant with Garlic Sauce and the Sauté Wonderful Chicken in less than 15 minutes. This feat can be reproduced at home, but only if your wok is properly heated beforehand and you have all your ingredients and utensils within easy reach. We urge you to memorize the recipes before beginning.

Note: *The "chili sauce" called for in each of these recipes is prepared from fresh red peppers, dried hot peppers, sesame oil, salt and cooking wine. It may be purchased in a Chinese grocery, or you may make it at home, by combining the ingredients to suit your taste. Grind the fresh red peppers with the dry peppers. Then add oil, salt and wine. Mix well. To prepare the "cornstarch paste," combine 1 part cornstarch with 2 parts cold water.*

HOT AND SPICY SHRIMP (SERVES 2)

    1 pound peeled fresh shrimp
    2 egg whites
    1 teaspoon cooking wine
    ⅙ teaspoon salt
    4 to 6 cups peanut or vegetable oil
 1½ tablespoons cornstarch

    ½ teaspoon minced garlic
    1 teaspoon chopped ginger root
    2 tablespoons ketchup
    1 tablespoon rice wine
    ¼ teaspoon chili sauce
    2 tablespoons sugar
    ⅙ teaspoon salt
    1 tablespoon chicken broth
    1 tablespoon cornstarch paste
    2 tablespoons chopped green scallions
    1 teaspoon sesame oil
    2 drops vinegar

Marinate shrimp in mixture of egg white, wine, salt, 1 tablespoon oil and 1½ tablespoons cornstarch for 15 minutes.

Deep-fry shrimp in boiling oil. When the shrimp turn white
(about 90-percent done), remove and drain oil from pan or wok.

Put back 2 tablespoons of oil in pan or wok. Sauté minced garlic and chopped ginger for a few seconds. Stir in ketchup, rice
wine, chili sauce, sugar and salt. Add shrimp and chicken broth,
stirring constantly. Stir with cornstarch paste, and then add
chopped green scallions. Stir in sesame oil and vinegar. Serve.

SAUTÉ WONDERFUL CHICKEN (SERVES 2)

1 egg
1½ tablespoons cornstarch
¼ teaspoon salt
1 pound chicken meat, diced

3 cups vegetable oil
2 cups diced Chinese cabbage

½ teaspoon minced ginger
1 tablespoon chopped scallions
1 tablespoon soy sauce
½ teaspoon vinegar
½ teaspoon rice wine
  pinch MSG
¼ teaspoon sugar
1 tablespoon cornstarch paste
1 teaspoon chicken or pork broth

1 tablespoon oil
1 teaspoon chili sauce
¾ cup ground peanuts
1 teaspoon sesame oil

Combine egg, cornstarch and salt. Marinate chicken in this mixture for a few minutes.

Heat oil in wok until it begins to boil. Add chicken and fry, stirring constantly, for 2 minutes. Add cabbage and continue to fry for another ½ minute. Remove from oil and drain. Remove oil from wok.

Combine ginger, scallions, soy sauce, vinegar, wine, MSG, sugar, cornstarch paste and broth to form a sauce. Mix well.

Heat 1 tablespoon oil in wok. Add chili sauce and sauté for a few seconds. Add chicken and cabbage, then peanuts. Mix well, then add sauce. Cook all together for a minute or two, stirring constantly. Stir in sesame oil and serve.

EGGPLANT WITH GARLIC SAUCE (SERVES 2)

1 pound eggplant
3 to 4 cups vegetable oil

1½ tablespoons minced ginger
2 tablespoons chopped scallions
1 tablespoon minced garlic
2 tablespoons soy sauce
2 tablespoons vinegar
1½ teaspoons MSG
2 tablespoons cornstarch paste

3 tablespoons oil
1 to 2 tablespoons chili sauce
½ pound ground pork, boiled and drained

Peel eggplant and cut lengthwise into ½-inch slices. Then cut into strips about ½ inch wide.

Heat oil in wok until boiling. Add eggplant and fry until soft (about 5 minutes). Remove eggplant from oil and drain. Squeeze out oil from the eggplant. Remove oil from wok.

Combine ginger, scallions, garlic, soy sauce, vinegar, MSG and cornstarch paste to form a sauce.

Heat 3 tablespoons oil in wok. Add chili sauce and heat for a few seconds. Stir in ground pork, then add eggplant. Stir. Now add sauce and stir well. Sauté for 2 minutes. Serve.

SZECHUAN TASTE

23 CHATHAM SQUARE
NEW YORK CITY
267-0672

Szechuan Taste is an eye-catching restaurant, dramatically oc-cupying one of the many corners that converge to form Chatham Square. The interior is light and spacious, adorned with thriving spider plants and Vera Chow's bold, Orientally inspired abstract paintings. Vera is owner Robert Chow's wife; together they form a charming, worldly, enterprising—and successful—couple. Mr. Chow, who was trained as a biochemist, came to America in 1962, traveling the common route of part-time work in various Chinese restaurants before opening Szechuan Taste in 1970. He now has at least four restaurants to his name, including one in Flatbush, Brooklyn. Mrs. Chow teaches fine arts at a New York high school, doubling during the evening as hostess in the restaurants.

TAI CHIEN CHICKEN (SERVES 2)

This dish was originated by the chef of Chang Tai Chien, "the Oriental Picasso."

10 ounces boneless chicken in bite-size pieces
2 egg yolks
3 cups vegetable oil
2 stalks celery, in ¼-inch diagonal slices
¼ large onion
½ green or red pepper, in bite-size pieces

1 tablespoon sherry
2 tablespoons soy sauce
1 tablespoon sweet rice (see recipe, p. 284)
1 teaspoon sugar
2 tablespoons cornstarch dissolved in ½ cup water

2 teaspoons chopped scallion
1 teaspoon finely chopped ginger
½ teaspoon finely chopped garlic
1 tablespoon hot red peppers

Combine chicken pieces with egg yolk. Heat oil in wok until it is boiling. Add chicken pieces and deep-fry for 5 minutes, stirring occasionally. Add vegetables and cook another ½ minute. Remove vegetables and chicken from oil and drain.

Pour off most of the oil, leaving only enough for sautéing. Combine sherry, soy sauce, sweet rice, sugar and dissolved cornstarch to form a sauce. Put scallions, ginger, garlic and peppers in wok and sauté for 1 or 2 minutes. Add vegetables, chicken and sauce. Stir well and heat thoroughly. Serve.

SLICED PORK WITH GARLIC SAUCE (SERVES 2)

½ pound boiled fresh ham, in very thin slices
1 part hot oil to 2 parts soy sauce
  chopped ginger
  chopped garlic
  chopped scallions
  crushed red peppers
  sugar

Chill ham. Combine ingredients for sauce, using proportions to taste, and pour over meat just before serving.

CHINESE CABBAGE CASSEROLE (SERVES 2 TO 4)

1 pound Chinese cabbage, in 1- or 2-inch pieces
¼ cup boned, diced chicken
¼ cup small shrimp, peeled and deveined
¼ cup diced ham
¼ cup black mushrooms
4 pork meatballs (about 1 inch in diameter, prepared from
    ground pork and egg)
¼ cup green peas
4 cups clear chicken broth

Cover bottom of heavy saucepan with cabbage. Place remaining solid ingredients in little mounds on top of the cabbage. Cover with clear chicken broth, cover pot and simmer for 15 minutes. Season with salt and sherry before serving.

Mrs. Keung, the owner's mother, rests in the window of Tai Fung Lau.

TAI FUNG LAU

116 COURT STREET
BROOKLYN
625-8878

Located in a rather unlikely spot on Court Street in Brooklyn, Tai Fung Lau is among the city's better Szechuan restaurants. We watched in awe as Peter Keung prepared the following dishes for us in his kitchen, and we recommend them as simple, delicious introductions to the niceties of Chinese cooking. The Tai Fung Lau kitchen is a paragon of efficiency, with countless small bowls filled with vegetables and meats sliced, shredded or cubed for quick cooking. There is also an assortment of bowls holding soy sauce, hot sauce, cornstarch, chicken broth, sherry, etc., plus the huge wok, black and shiny from constant use. To make any of these dishes at home, you need the patience and perseverance to cut all the ingredients to their proper sizes, the organization to arrange everything so that it is at hand when you are cooking, and a very hot wok. In choosing a soy sauce, stay away from the popular American brands and ask your nearest Chinese grocer for a soy sauce from the mainland—and specify that you will be using it for sautéing.

SHREDDED BEEF HOME STYLE (SERVES 2)

3 cups peanut or vegetable oil
1 cup carrots, in narrow strips
1 cup celery, in narrow strips
1 cup bamboo shoots, in narrow strips

1 pound flank steak, cut into very small strips

¼ cup chicken stock

¼ cup soy sauce

2 tablespoons sherry

2 teaspoons minced ginger

2 teaspoons minced garlic

1 teaspoon hot pepper sauce

1 tablespoon sweet rice

1 tablespoon cornstarch dissolved in ¼ cup cold water

2 teaspoons sesame oil

½ cup chopped scallions

Heat wok thoroughly. Pour in peanut or vegetable oil and heat it until it begins to steam. Gently add vegetables and beef and cook over high heat until nearly done (about 3 to 5 minutes). Remove from oil and drain. Pour off oil from wok.

Combine remaining ingredients (except scallions) in wok and heat a few minutes. Add beef and vegetables and sauté several minutes longer.

Garnish with chopped scallions and serve immediately.

In the restaurant, of course, the stock used is Tai Fung Lau's own rich broth obtained from boiling various bones for many hours. You might do the same, or you can get away with some canned stock or bouillon.

Sweet rice, which is used as a flavoring in only small quantities, is rather difficult to make and use at home, since it keeps for only a few days. However, here's how to do it:

½ pound white rice

⅛ Chinese yeast ball

⅛ cup white flour

Soak rice in warm water for 3 or 4 hours. Steam until done, then drain and rinse with cold water. Break yeast ball into a powder. Combine with rice and flour. Cover and keep in a warm place for 1 or 2 days. Use sparingly in this dish and the following one.

DOUBLE COOKED SAUTÉED PORK (SERVES 2)

3 cups peanut oil
1 pound fresh ham, thinly sliced in 1×2-inch pieces
½ cup bamboo shoots, sliced
2 green peppers, cut into ½-inch triangles
2 cups Chinese cabbage, in rectangles or triangles

¼ cup stock
3 tablespoons soy sauce
3 tablespoons sherry
1 tablespoon sweet rice
2 teaspoons minced ginger
2 teaspoons minced garlic
1 teaspoon hot sauce
2 teaspoons sesame oil
6 tablespoons hoy sin sauce
½ cup chopped scallions
1 tablespoon cornstarch dissolved in ¼ cup water

Heat wok. Add oil and heat thoroughly. Add ham and vegetables, and fry quickly for a few minutes until vegetables are almost cooked. Remove from oil, drain, and pour off oil.

Combine remaining ingredients in wok and heat. Add ham and vegetables, and cook a few minutes longer. Adjust seasoning and serve.

MU SHU PORK

PANCAKES (MAKES 10 TO 15 PANCAKES)

½ pound flour
  approximately ¼ cup hot water
  rendered pork fat

Slowly add hot water to flour and blend well. Knead dough until it is smooth and satiny. Dough should not be at all sticky.

On a floured board, roll dough into a cylinder about 1 inch
thick. Slice into 1-inch sections. Flatten each section, using a
wide knife or the heel of your hand.

Press 2 flattened sections together, putting just a bit of pork
fat between them. Do this with all the sections.

Roll out each double section into a 6-inch circle. Bake pancakes on cookie sheets in a 350° oven or on a hot griddle, just
until they begin to brown (about 2 minutes).

Fold pancakes into quarters and refrigerate until ready to
serve. At that time, steam over hot water.

FILLING (FILLS 4 TO 6 PANCAKES, TO SERVE 2)

  3 cups peanut or vegetable oil
  1 pound pork, shredded into very thin strips
  3 eggs, beaten lightly
  1 4-ounce can bamboo shoots, in strips
  1 cup shredded cloud ears
  2 cups shredded Chinese cabbage
  3 scallions, shredded
  3 tablespoons soy sauce
1½ tablespoons sherry

2 teaspoons sesame oil
⅛ teaspoon black pepper

Heat wok. Add oil, and heat thoroughly. Add pork and cook 1 or 2 minutes, until almost done. Remove from oil and drain.

Slip beaten eggs into oil and let cook, stirring briskly and shredding the eggs. Remove from oil and drain. Pour off most of oil, leaving only enough to sauté vegetables.

Add vegetables and sauté 3 or 4 minutes. Add pork and eggs and cook several minutes longer, adding soy sauce, sherry, sesame oil and pepper after a minute or two. Continue stirring until everything is covered with sauce and thoroughly cooked.

Place a few tablespoons of filling in center of each pancake. Roll cake around filling and eat with your hands.

HONEY APPLES (SERVES 2)

½ cup sugar
½ cup water
¼ cup cornstarch
¼ cup flour
    cold water
1 apple, skinned and cut into ½-inch cubes
    clean vegetable oil for deep frying

Heat sugar and water over low heat until sugar becomes stringy.

Combine cornstarch and flour with cold water until you have a thick, creamy batter.

Dip apple cubes in the batter and deep-fry in very hot oil. Fry until apples rise to surface and coating looks crisp. It will not turn brown, so don't wait for it to do so.

Drain fried apples and place in small bowls surrounded by ice cubes. Cover with sugar syrup and serve.

LA TAZA DE ORO

96 EIGHTH AVENUE
NEW YORK CITY
243-9946

Open since 1947, this inconspicuous but distinctive luncheonette offers standard Puerto Rican fare at modest prices and in an atmosphere of genuine warmth. The food is solid, tasty and plentiful. The Carne Guisada (beef stew) is typical of La Taza de Oro's repertoire and is an excellent dish for home meals. Octopus Salad is a refreshing surprise.

OCTOPUS SALAD (SERVES 4)

1 pound octopus
2 tablespoons garlic sauce (prepared from minced garlic, oil, vinegar and salt, mixed to taste and refrigerated)
½ cup finely chopped green pepper
½ cup finely chopped onion
few drops Tabasco
2 tablespoons oil
1 tablespoon vinegar
1 teaspoon oregano

Boil octopus until tender (about 2 hours). Drain and rinse with cold water. Remove skin and cut into small pieces (about ½-inch cubes or smaller).

Combine octopus with remaining ingredients. Mix well and marinate at least one day in refrigerator.

CARNE GUISADA (SERVES 4)

1 pound beef (bottom round) in 1-inch cubes
2 or 3 onions, in quarters
2 green peppers, in quarters
4 cloves garlic, minced
10 stuffed olives
2 tablespoons chopped fresh cilantro
2 teaspoons salt
1 16-ounce can tomato purée

2 potatoes, quartered
1 tablespoon prepared achiote
2 teaspoons oregano
½ teaspoon pepper

2 tablespoons cornstarch dissolved in ½ cup cold water

Place beef, onions, peppers, garlic, olives, cilantro and salt in a heavy saucepan. Cover with tomato purée. Bring to a boil, cover and simmer until beef is tender (about 1½ hours). Add water if necessary. Add potatoes, achiote, oregano and pepper, and simmer another 45 minutes. Thicken sauce with cornstarch mixture and serve.

TEXAS TACO

From pushcart to hole-in-the-wall stand to restaurant was the path traversed by Rosemary Jamison's Texas Taco enterprise, an imaginative venture sparked by Rosemary's lively personality and cooking skill. The restaurant was set up in a unique cafeteria style: scattered around a barnlike room were several gaily decorated pushcarts, each offering a different specialty of the house. The check which you picked up at the entrance was punched for each item selected, and your money was collected at the door. The atmosphere was informal and comfortable, with constant chatter provided by a lively talking parrot.

Unfortunately, the business folded; Rosemary has left the New York scene, though her recipes survive.

FRIED CHICKEN LIVERS (SERVES 2 TO 4)

2 eggs
5 tablespoons flour
2 tablespoons water
¼ teaspoon salt
  pinch of sugar
¼ teaspoon pepper
1 pound chicken livers, blotted dry on paper towels
  Crisco for deep frying

"Beat eggs and add flour slowly, until mixture resembles sticky bubble gum. Add water, beating constantly, until the consistency of Elmer's Glue is achieved. Add salt, sugar, and so much pepper it looks like too much. Dip livers in batter and deep-fry in hot Crisco until golden. Watch out for popping grease. Serve with mustard and duck sauce."

BURRITOS (SERVES 4)

1 pound ground beef
1 tablespoon water
   salt
1 dozen flour tortillas, steamed
   chili powder
½ cup dehydrated chopped onions, mixed with hot water
¾ cup grated sharp old English cheese
¾ cup mashed pinto or kidney beans
   Frank's Louisiana Hot Sauce

Crisco for deep frying

Sauté beef with water and salt to taste until it is gray.

In center of each tortilla, place 1½ tablespoons beef. Sprinkle with chili powder. Add 2 teaspoons onions, 1 tablespoon cheese, 1 tablespoon beans. Add some hot sauce to taste. Roll tortilla into a packet and secure with toothpicks. Using tongs, dip into hot oil (350°) until golden. Drain and serve.

TIP TOP

1489 SECOND AVENUE
NEW YORK CITY
650-0723

Tip Top is among the most pleasant restaurants in New York. It looks very much like a simple luncheonette, but the food is outstanding and the atmosphere extraordinarily relaxing. Margaret and Gabriel Keszely, the owners, were formerly bookkeepers in Hungary. Now Margaret does all the cooking in a neat and well-equipped kitchen, while her husband takes care of the service. The food is well prepared and served in large portions. The Keszelys take great pride in their restaurant, and their care is transmitted to the customer.

The recipes for Chicken Paprikash, Chicken Giblet Soup and Liver Noodles are complementary—each requires a different part of 2 2½-pound frying chickens. The Palacsinta are delicious.

CHICKEN PAPRIKASH (SERVES 4)

       1 onion, chopped
       3 tablespoons vegetable oil
       4 chicken legs, wings and breasts (from 2 2½-pound frying
           chickens)
      ¾ tomato, chopped
    1½ green peppers, chopped
       2 teaspoons paprika
       1 teaspoon salt
         water

1 cup sour cream
2 tablespoons flour

Sauté onions in oil just until they become translucent. Add chicken, remaining vegetables, seasonings and water until chicken is ¾ covered. Cover pot and simmer for ½ hour.

Remove chicken and vegetables from sauce. Strain liquid and mix about half of it with sour cream, flour and 2 tablespoons water. Serve over chicken with Egg Noodles (see below).

EGG NOODLES (SERVES 4)

2 teaspoons salt
2 eggs
½ pound flour
  water

Add 1 teaspoon salt and eggs to flour. Mix well. Slowly add water until you have a soft dough.

Heat water in a large pot until boiling. Add 1 teaspoon salt. Cut bite-size pieces of dough and drop into boiling water. Boil for a few minutes and serve.

(You may use a noodle machine, available at Paprikas Weiss Importers, 1546 Second Avenue, to cut dough.)

CHICKEN GIBLET SOUP (SERVES 4)

  necks, backs, hearts, gizzards, from 2 2½-pound frying
    chickens
1½ quarts water

1 teaspoon salt
1 parsley root, diced
1 stalk celery, diced
1 carrot, diced
½ green pepper, diced
½ tomato, diced
½ cup sliced mushrooms (optional)
   handful chopped parsley
2 tablespoons oil
1 tablespoon flour
   paprika

Cut giblets into bite-size pieces. Combine in pot with water, salt and vegetables. Simmer, covered, for ½ hour.

Heat oil and slowly stir in flour. Add a dash of paprika. Add to soup and stir in well. Add Liver Noodles (see below) and simmer another few minutes. Serve.

LIVER NOODLES

1 egg, beaten
1 tablespoon oil
1 tablespoon flour
1 tablespoon bread crumbs
2 chicken livers, cut into fine pieces
   salt
   pepper
2 teaspoons chopped parsley

Combine all ingredients. Using a spoon, drop small pieces of mixture into boiling soup (after flour has been added). Let boil for 2 to 3 minutes and serve.

PALACSINTA (SERVES 4)

⅓ cup water
⅓ cup milk
⅓ cup Seven-Up
 1 large egg, beaten
⅔ cup sifted flour
¼ teaspoon vanilla extract
¾ teaspoon sugar
⅛ teaspoon salt

   vegetable oil

Beat all ingredients (except oil) to form a smooth, light batter.
Heat a 5- or 6-inch skillet. Grease liberally with vegetable oil.
Add batter just to cover bottom of skillet. Cook over high heat.
Add a little more oil along the sides, turn Palacsinta, and brown
on second side.

Serve Palacsinta rolled around one of the following: ground
poppy seeds and sugar; ground walnuts and sugar; apricot jam; a
mixture of cottage cheese, sugar, lemon juice and egg yolk.
Sprinkle with confectioner's sugar.

VICTORIA CHINA

2532 BROADWAY
NEW YORK CITY
865-1810

Chinese-Cuban food has become a West Side standby, and the Victoria China is an excellent example of this popular restaurant style. The term Chinese-Cuban, or "comidas chinas y criollas," refers not to a blend of styles, but to the offering of both Latin and Chinese food side by side. Surprisingly, the two go quite well together. The repertoire in each restaurant of this genre is basically the same, so variations in quality are easy to discern —and the Victoria China merits a high rating for nearly all its preparations, if not for its atmosphere. The Congee, listed on the Latin side of the menu, is an unusual dish, different from the standard Chinese preparation, but apparently derivative. Black Beans need no introduction.

CHOPPED BEEF (SERVES 2 TO 4)

This is a very tasty way to prepare chopped meat. It's excellent served with rice and vegetables (or beans), it's cheap and it's easy.

1 pound ground beef
1 large onion, chopped
1 large green pepper, chopped
3 to 5 cloves garlic, minced
2 to 3 tablespoons vegetable oil
⅓ cup sherry

⅓ cup water
½ of 6-ounce can tomato paste
2 bay leaves
½ teaspoon salt
¼ teaspoon cumin
⅛ teaspoon white pepper
dash of Tabasco

Heat beef in frying pan, breaking into pieces and cooking until almost fully browned. Place in strainer and rinse thoroughly to remove all grease. Drain.

Sauté onions, peppers and garlic in oil until onions are golden. Add beef and mix well. Add sherry, water, tomato paste and bay leaves. Sprinkle with salt, cumin and white pepper. Simmer 5 or 10 minutes, stirring well. Season with Tabasco before serving.

BLACK OR RED BEANS (SERVES 6 TO 8)

1 pound black (or red) beans
½ pound beef or pork bones
1 chorizo

2 tablespoons olive oil
1 large green pepper, chopped very fine
1 large onion, chopped very fine
4 cloves garlic, minced
2 teaspoons salt
1½ teaspoons cumin
2 bay leaves

Soak beans overnight in water twice as deep as beans. Drain and rinse. Place in large, heavy pot and cover with water 1 inch above level of beans. Add bones and chorizo. Bring to a boil and simmer, covered, 2½ hours, until beans are soft.

Heat olive oil in a skillet and sauté peppers and onions with garlic, salt, cumin and bay leaves. Cook gently until onions are golden and mixture is very aromatic. Add to beans, mix thoroughly and simmer another 10 minutes. Serve.

SHRIMPS IN VINEGAR (SERVES 4 TO 6)

1 pound shrimp
½ cup vinegar
2 to 3 tablespoons olive oil
1 teaspoon salt
¼ to ½ teaspoon sugar
½ cup very finely chopped green pepper
½ cup very finely chopped onion
½ cup very finely chopped sour pickle
1 teaspoon very finely chopped garlic

Clean and butterfly shrimp. Boil for about 2 minutes, then rinse in cold water.

Combine vinegar, oil, salt, sugar, green pepper, onion, pickles and garlic. Add shrimp and mix well. Adjust seasoning to taste. Chill.

CONGEE (SERVES 4)

1 cup rice
¾ pound beef or shrimp, cut into small pieces
2 onions, chopped fine
1 green pepper, chopped fine
2 tablespoons oil

    salt
½ cup tomato paste
 1 cup water
    sherry
    soy sauce

Wash rice and boil in 3 times the usual amount of water just until rice is soft.

Sauté beef (or shrimp), onions and pepper in vegetable oil. When onions are golden, season with salt. Add tomato paste, water and a dash each of sherry and soy sauce. Simmer for 10 to 15 minutes, then combine with rice and serve as a soup.

VINCENT PETROSINO'S SEAFOOD RESTAURANT AND FISH MARKET

100 GREENWICH STREET (NEAR RECTOR)
227-5398

This is a bustling, no-nonsense seafood restaurant run by Vincent Petrosino, a master of his trade. Neither the decor nor the service is memorable, but the food is outstanding—thanks to the high quality of the fresh fish (which may be purchased at a retail counter in the front of the restaurant) and the simplicity of preparation.

The following two recipes are wonderfully easy, and surprisingly delicious.

SHRIMP STEW (SERVES 2 TO 4)

   1 pound shrimp, shelled and deveined
1½ quarts water
   2 cups milk
   2 tablespoons butter (or more, if desired)
  ½ teaspoon salt
  ⅛ teaspoon pepper
  ⅛ teaspoon paprika

Boil shrimp in 1½ quarts water for 8 minutes. Drain and conserve broth. Place shrimp in bowls.

Heat milk, adding butter and ½ cup shrimp broth. Season with salt, pepper and paprika. Pour over shrimp and serve.

FISH CHOWDER (SERVES 4)

2 pounds in all of cod, halibut and salmon (in any proportions)
1 stalk celery, sliced
1½ quarts water
2 tablespoons cornstarch dissolved in ½ cup milk
salt
pepper
cracker meal

Boil fish with celery in water until fish is tender. Remove fish from broth and pick out bones. Return to broth. Add milk-and-cornstarch mixture to thicken. Stir in well. Season with salt and pepper, and add cracker meal. Serve.

Z

117 EAST 15TH STREET
NEW YORK CITY
254-0960

A thoroughly pleasant place, Z offers an interesting list of Greek specialties. The recipes we gathered are robustly spiced delicacies, notably free of the fattiness that is often an integral characteristic of Greek food. The Spetsoda is especially good and is a traditional Greek fisherman's dish. As owner Rigas Kappatos explained, the dish appears in numerous forms throughout the Greek isles, with the fish varying with the day's catch and the sauce concocted from "whatever is around." It's a sensitive and wonderfully aromatic way to prepare fish.

EXOHIKO (SERVES 8)

1 cup olive oil
2 small onions, chopped
1 bunch scallions, chopped
5 pounds leg of lamb, in ½-inch cubes
1 tablespoon flour
2 cups red wine
⅛ teaspoon black pepper
2 tablespoons fresh chopped dill
½ pound butter
1 16-ounce can sweet peas
⅔ 16-ounce can diced carrots
½ pound feta or kefalotyri cheese
1 pound filo

In a large saucepan, heat oil and brown onions and scallions. Add meat and flour, and brown meat well on all sides. If the lamb is not very fatty, add about ¾ cup water. Add wine and pepper and simmer gently 20 to 30 minutes, until sauce is thickened and meat is almost done.

Remove meat from stove and let cool thoroughly. Add fresh dill and mix well.

Melt butter, drain peas and carrots, and break the cheese into small pieces. Carefully lay out a sheet of filo and brush lightly with butter. Place a second sheet over this one and brush again with butter. Repeat the process with a third sheet. Now place ⅛ of the meat mixture on the dough, centered and a few inches from the near edge. Sprinkle with carrots, peas and cheese. Fold both sides of the dough over the filling, fold the edge up and roll, creating a large rectangular packet. Brush well with butter and place in a buttered baking dish.

Repeat this process until you have 8 packets, being sure to handle the filo gently—it tears rather easily. Bake in a 350° oven for 30 minutes, or until the cheese is melted and the filo is golden and crisp.

SPETSODA (SERVES 4)

¾ cup olive oil
1 onion, chopped
1 stalk celery, chopped
4 tablespoons tomato paste diluted in 3 cups water
½ cup white wine
3 bay leaves
½ teaspoon salt
⅛ teaspoon black pepper
1 tablespoon fresh chopped parsley

3 pounds snapper, cod or scrod, cut in thick slices
5 cloves garlic, minced
2 or 3 canned tomatoes, split into halves
1 fresh tomato, sliced thin

Heat olive oil. Sauté onion and celery until onion is golden.

Add tomato paste and water to sautéed vegetables. Add wine, bay leaves, salt, pepper and parsley. Stir well. Simmer gently 30 to 40 minutes, until sauce thickens. (You may add a tablespoon or two of flour.) Strain sauce through a food mill.

Arrange fish in a buttered baking dish and cover with sauce. Sprinkle minced garlic on each slice of fish, then lay the split canned tomatoes over the garlic and top finally with slices of fresh tomato.

Bake in 400° oven for 20 minutes.

MELITZANOSALATA (EGGPLANT SALAD) (SERVES 4 TO 8)

2 eggplants
1 tablespoon chopped fresh dill
5 cloves garlic
1 onion
  juice of ½ lemon
3 tablespoons mayonnaise
  salt

Bake eggplants until very soft. Remove skin and some of the seeds. Pass the eggplant pulp through a grinder.

Pass the dill, garlic and onion through a grinder.

Beat eggplant, dill, garlic, onion, lemon juice and mayonnaise until creamy. Add salt to taste. Chill and serve on toast or crackers.

GLOSSARY OF UNUSUAL INGREDIENTS

ACHIOTE   the orange-red seeds of the annato tree, used in place of saffron to color rice yellow

AGAR-AGAR   an Oriental form of gelatin

AMAR DIN   sheets of dried apricots, found in Greek or Middle Eastern groceries

BEAN CURD CAKES (tofu)   squares of soft white curd made from soybean milk; sold canned or fresh in Oriental stores

BLACK CLAMS   conches from Ecuador; sold canned

BULGUR   a cracked-wheat product available in bulk

CHORIZOS   Spanish-style sausages, available in Spanish groceries

CILANTRO   fresh coriander leaves, used widely in Spanish and Chinese cooking

CIPPOLINI   small wild onions

CLOUD EARS   large, thick mushrooms used in Chinese cooking; sold dried

DAIKON   a type of large white radish used in Japanese cooking

FILO   a very thin pastry dough, sold generally in 1-pound packages; available at Middle Eastern groceries.

GABI   a Philippine fruit, occasionally available in Philippine groceries

GUANABANA (soursop)   a large tropical fruit with soft white flesh

HOI SIN SAUCE   a thick brownish-red sauce used in flavoring certain Chinese dishes

JACKFRUIT   a tropical fruit found in southern Florida; yields a sweet or acid juice with a strong bananalike flavor

KOMBU   a thick, flat seaweed used for flavoring stock; sold dried

MAMEY   the fruit of a tropical tree with a bright yellow juicy flesh

MANDIOCA FLOUR   a flour made from the mandioc root

ÑAME   a tropical yam

NORI   a thin, flat edible seaweed; sold dried

OYSTER SAUCE   a bottled dark brown sauce made from oysters and brine, used in small amounts to flavor meat and vegetable dishes in Chinese cooking

PANCETTA   Italian bacon, sold in Italian meat markets

SANSHO   xanthoxylum seeds, available in Japanese food markets

SPAETZLE   a type of egg noodle

STRUDEL DOUGH   see filo

TAGLIARINI   a form of pasta

TAHINI   sesame paste

TAMARI   a special type of soy sauce, aged longer than usual and with no chemical additives

TOMATILLOS VERDES   whole green Spanish tomatoes

UNTO   a form of pork fat, available in Spanish meat markets

YAUTÍA   the starchy root of a tropical plant; the flesh is creamy white and similar in flavor to a mealy Idaho potato

YUCA   the tuber of a tropical plant, similar to a potato

INDEX OF RECIPES

Note: In addition to the usual entries, recipes of foreign ancestry also appear under the nationality or region from which they have been adapted.

Adobo (meat in spicy sauce):
  Chicken, 74–75
  Pork, 53
Appetizers and snacks:
  Baba Ghanouj, 82–83, 202–03
  Bourek, 118
  Chommos, 224
  dim sum as, *see under* Dim sum
  Empanadas, 252–53
  Enchiladas Suizas, 185–86
  Fool Mudamas, 223
  Fried Cippolini, 248
  Lumpia Frito, 75–76
  Lupinis, 247
  Melitzanosalata, 304
  Moules Ravigote, 218
  Pâté Maison, 217–18
  Pirogi, 177–78
  Samosa, 268–69
  Shrimps in Vinegar, 298
  Skodalia, 146
  Spinach Pie (Spanakotiropita),
    144–45
Apple(s):
  Cobbler, 233–34
  Crunch, 214
  as filling for cobblers, 234
  as filling for crêpes, 57–58
  Honey, 287
Apple Noodle Pudding, 179
Apple Strudel, 102–03
Argentine dishes:
  Empanadas, 252–53
  Matambre, 254
Austrian dishes, *see* Viennese dishes

Baba Ghanouj (chopped eggplant
  with tahini, spices), 82–83, 202–
  203

Bacalão Gomez de Sa (salt cod with
  potatoes, onions), 63–64
Baked Gefulte Fish, 127–28
Baklava (filo, pistachio nuts), 48
Bananas, Fried, 45
  see also Plantains
Barley Mushroom Soup, 126–27
Barley Soup with Beef and Mush-
  rooms, 231
Basic Pastry Dough (for Danishes),
  119–20
Batido (cold tropical fruit-milk
  drink), 156–57
Beans:
  Black or Red (Cuban style), 297–
    298
  Cassoulet Toulousaine, 220–21
  in Feijoada Completa, 72–73
  Fool Mudamas, 223
  Galician Bean Soup, 180–81
  Lupinis, 247
  Pasta e Fagiole, 246
  see also Black beans; Chick peas;
    Lentils; White beans
Bean Sprout Salad, 263
Beef:
  Boliche, 227–28
  Boti Kebab, 270
  Bourguignon, 219–20
  Brisket of, 59–60
  Bul Go Ki, 205
  Burritos, 291
  Carne Guisada, 289
  Carolina Beef Stew, 164–65
  Chopped, 296–97
  Churrasco Gaucho, 68
  in Congee, 298–99
  Empanadas, 252–53
  Feijoada Completa, 72–73
  Filet Mignon Ideal, 158